GREAT PRO RUNNING BACKS

Edited and with an Introduction by
LUD DUROSKA

Written by members of *The New York Times* Sports Staff

GROSSET & DUNLAP • Publishers • New York
A National General Company

Library of Congress Catalog Card Number: 73—821
ISBN: 0-448-11501-2 (Trade Edition)
ISBN: 0-448-03930-3 (Library Edition)
Copyright © 1973 by Lud Duroska.
All rights reserved under International and Pan-American Copyright Conventions.
Published simultaneously in Canada. Printed in the United States of America.

*Dedicated with love to
Nannette, Eileen and Amy*

Acknowledgment

The help of the PR directors of the National Football League teams for whom the great pro running backs starred, or star, was greatly appreciated, as was the assistance of Joe Browne and Kay O'Reilly of Commissioner Pete Rozelle's staff.

Thanks to Jim Campbell of the Pro Football Hall of Fame and John Looney, who did yeoman's service in photo research.

All records were supplied by the Elias Sports Bureau, official statisticians for the National Football League.

Contents

Introduction *Lud Duroska*	8
JIM THORPE *Arthur Daley*	10
RED GRANGE *Joseph Durso*	20
BRONKO NAGURSKI *Lud Duroska*	30
STEVE VAN BUREN *Murray Chass*	40
HUGH McELHENNY *Parton Keese*	50
PAUL HORNUNG *Joseph Durso*	60
JIM TAYLOR *Thomas Rogers*	70
JIM BROWN *George DeGregorio*	80
GALE SAYERS *William N. Wallace*	96
LEROY KELLY *Marty Ralbovsky*	106
FLOYD LITTLE *Parton Keese*	116
LARRY CSONKA *Marty Ralbovsky*	126
LARRY BROWN *Murray Chass*	136
O. J. SIMPSON *George DeGregorio*	146

GREAT PRO
RUNNING BACKS

Introduction

The feats of the great pro running backs, who range in chronological order from Jim Thorpe to O. J. Simpson, are depicted graphically in word and picture on the pages that follow. But, interestingly, if it had not been for a young English student named William Webb Ellis and for the stubbornness of Harvard University, there likely would not be any running backs, and fans today would have been deprived of the pleasure of watching such star performers as Larry Csonka crashing through the line, or O. J. feinting his way past a defensive back, or Larry Brown smoothly sidestepping a tackler. A grim thought.

For several centuries football was a loosely organized, any-number-to-a-side, soccer-type game played in England. Its name was descriptive of its principal action: foot (kicking) ball. Then, late one November afternoon, the first running back suddenly materialized. His impetuous deed is engraved on a tablet at Rugby School that reads:

This Stone

Commemorates the Exploit of

WILLIAM WEBB ELLIS

Who with a fine disregard of the rules of

Football, as played in his time,

First took the ball in his arms and ran with it,

Thus originating the distinctive feature of

The Rugby Game

A. D. 1823

What possessed Ellis to break with tradition is unknown. The story is told that, according to the custom at the private secondary school, a game ended when the five o'clock bell sounded. The bell had just begun to toll when Ellis caught a punt. With only a few seconds left and with the score tied, perhaps, he probably wanted desperately to score a goal. In his desire, he forgot the rules. Instead of taking a free kick, Ellis tucked the ball under his arm and raced with "reckless abandon" down the field and across the goal line. His teammates and opponents were shocked at his folly and undoubtedly his "touchdown" was called back.

Later, the other players reconsidered. They began to realize the exciting possibilities in advancing the ball with running maneuvers. And so the game of Rugby was born—fittingly named after Ellis's alma mater, scene of the first run.

Surprisingly, Americans were slow in learning the new game from their English cousins, and when they finally did, Harvard deserves credit. Football in this country through much of the 19th century remained a kicking game. Historians have marked November 6, 1869, when Princeton and Rutgers met for the first time at New Brunswick, New Jersey, as the beginning of intercollegiate football competition. It seems to be a premature date for the ushering-in of a new era in a sport. The Rutgers-Princeton contest, with 25 men on each team, was played under soccer rules, meaning that running with the ball was prohibited. More properly, the meeting at New Brunswick should be regarded as the start of intercollegiate soccer.

During the next three years Columbia and Yale fielded teams and participated in games with Rutgers and Princeton, but they were still basically playing soccer. At the same time, Harvard students had devised a game they called the Boston Game, which was different in one very significant respect: A player was permitted to pick up the ball and run with it, provided he was being pursued.

In October, 1873, Harvard made an important decision that represents the turning point in the development of football in America. The Crimson refused an invitation to attend a convention in New York City with other Eastern colleges to prepare a code of rules and organize a league. Everybody else favored the soccer rules and, aware of that, Harvard stayed away, preferring to keep its Boston Game. If Harvard had decided to join the others, then soccer undeniably would have been firmly established as the collegiate sport.

Unable to schedule any games with its natural rivals because of the difference in rules, Harvard gladly accepted the challenge of McGill University of Montreal for two games at Cambridge in May, 1874. The first one was played under Harvard's rules and it won, 3 goals to 0. In the second game, which ended in a 0–0 tie, McGill introduced English Rugby (which allowed running with the ball at any time) to the United States. Rugby was an immediate hit with the Harvard players and they adopted its rules.

Rugby's popularity spread so rapidly that within two years Yale, Princeton, Columbia and Rutgers had their teams switch over to the rushing game. A new Intercollegiate Football Association, including Harvard this time, was formed.

By 1880, Walter Camp of Yale, who was to become known as the Father of American Football, was instrumental in making the first rule changes that altered the game irrevocably from Rugby and gave it its special American characteristics. From that point on, football evolved into the exciting sport we enjoy today. But if it had not been for Ellis and Harvard, who knows?

Lud Duroska

A ferocious tackler, the Canton Bulldogs' star (20) brings down Buffaloes' runner and forces a fumble in 1920 game at New York's Polo Grounds.

Jim Thorpe

Jim Thorpe

by Arthur Daley

When the selection committee of sportswriters assembled for the historic convocation that was to name the charter members to the Pro Football Hall of Fame, they were not fazed by the enormity of the task confronting them, even though it almost seemed presumptuous to sort out the best from the thousands of ancient heroes and the thousands of modern heroes. With painstaking care and constant questioning they began their assignment.

The man who was questioned most was the appointee from St. Louis, white-thatched Jimmy Conzelman, who had served as owner, coach and player in the National Football League. He had seen them all and his was the voice of authority. The youngest member of the committee, who had already established himself as a devil's advocate of sorts, kept turning to him continually. In preliminary discussions

Hall of Fame

Years after his retirement, he often gave half-time demonstrations of his skill at drop-kicking field goals.

he challenged the qualifications of one player after another. Then he suddenly was guilty of what the older committeemen had to regard as sheer sacrilege.

"Why all the fuss about Jim Thorpe?" he asked. "Everyone wants to railroad him into the Hall of Fame as if the No. 1 spot belongs to him by divine right. But I still have to be convinced. I never saw him play. In fact, I grew up in two-platoon with specialists in every position. Modern football is so superior to the football of Thorpe's day that I'm not even sure the old Indian could have made either platoon in modern ball. I'd like Jimmy Conzelman to clear that up for me. Jimmy, you played with Thorpe and you played against him. Could he have made either platoon on even the worst team in the league today?"

Conzelman pursed his lips as if the question were difficult. But his eyes danced as he thought back to the Sac and Fox Indian with the breathtaking skills, the man who had transformed the little Indian school at Carlisle, Pennsylvania, into a national collegiate power, and the man whose enormous prestige gave pro football the boost it so desperately needed in the early years.

"Yes," he said slowly, "Thorpe could have made the defensive platoon of the worst team in the league—and he also could have made it on the best team in the league. What's more, he would have been the best player on that platoon. He also could have made the offensive platoon of the worst team and the best one. He would have been the best player on that platoon. He would have been the best damn football player in the National Football League."

"I withdraw my objection," said the youngest committeeman.

That the big Indian should have been the first chosen is really of no deep significance because all are rated equals. In actuality, he was the last of the originals to be inducted because the order was determined by the alphabet. Sammy Baugh was first in. Jim Thorpe was last.

Even though only the legend of Jim Thorpe remains, he seems to many to be the most towering figure in the Hall of Fame. This is more than just a football player, you know. The Sac and Fox probably was the finest all-around athlete that America ever has produced.

Approximately half a century before the selection committee was meeting to weigh Thorpe and other gridiron immortals, an expert of different stature and background was offering an opinion of his own. He was King Gustaf V of Sweden, and he was aglow with admiration as he stood in front of the victory stand at the 1912 Olympic Games in Stockholm. Facing him was Jim Thorpe of the United States, winner of the supreme test at any Olympic Games, the grueling, exhausting decathlon.

"You, sir," said His Majesty, "are the greatest athlete in the world."

"Thanks, King," said the noble redman.

If the acceptance did not have the flowery grace that proper protocol demanded, it really didn't matter. The facts were essentially correct. What made them even more emphatic was that the big Indian also won the pentathlon, a five-event Olympic test, that has since been abandoned. The world's greatest athlete? You gotta believe it!

When the twentieth century reached its mid-point in 1950, the Associated Press polled sportswriters throughout the country to determine the No. 1 performer in each sport during the previous 50 years. Voting was close in some instances, but when it came to football it was no contest. Jim Thorpe won by a landslide.

The thunderous impact of the big Indian on the American public just cannot be visualized when placed among the more cynical standards of today. He was the prime folk hero in an era of folk heroes, so fabled a character that he could have served as a prototype for Frank Merriwell, a young man prodigiously skilled in every sport. There was one major difference. Merriwell was fictitious, Thorpe was fact.

Acknowledged by all was his position of eminence as the finest football player in the land. Undisputed was his extraordinary versatility as a track athlete. The 1912 Olympic Games proved it, even if the Sac and Fox was forced later to return his medals to the International Olympic Committee when charged with professionalism for innocently accepting $15 a week to play summer baseball. In time he became good enough to last eight seasons in the big leagues with the New York Giants, the Cincinnati Reds, and the Boston Braves. He shot golf in the 70's, bowled in the 200's, and was superb at lacrosse. He could box, wrestle, swim, shoot—there just was nothing in athletics beyond the ken of this magnificently endowed nature boy. He had size at 6 feet 1½ inches and 190 pounds. And he had blinding speed to go with it.

An almost parenthetical item concerns his high jumping. It is so illustrative of his agility and nimbleness. Not only did Thorpe win places on the Olympic team as a decathlon and pentathlon performer, but he also qualified as a high jumper, even if his high-jump entry was scratched at Stockholm. What height did he clear? He sailed over the bar at 6 feet 5 inches. And this was in 1912!

On a football field he could do everything. He blocked with the crumpling effect of a man chopping a cane stalk with a machete. He tackled with numbing force. When they gave Old Jim the ball, though, he was in his element. He had such speed and elusiveness that he was a wraith in an open field.

"I give 'em the hip," he once said in amusement, "and then I take it away."

Sometimes, though, he didn't take it

UPI
As an all-American performer at Carlisle.

15

away. He could throw that swivel hip at a tackler and actually knock him cold. He also had a straight arm that was as lethal as a Joe Louis jab. What made the big Indian so unusual, however, was that he was not limited to sweeping wide or slashing off tackle. He could splinter an enemy line with explosive bursts up the middle. Once he had the ball, he could strike anywhere.

He was an adequate enough passer in an era when there was little passing. But that also happened to be an era when the foot enjoyed a major place in football, and that was right down the Indian's alley. He may have been the strongest kicker ever. If not, he wasn't too far behind.

When he was performing for the Carlisle Indians against Lafayette College, then a top-ranking football power, his shortest punt measured 70 yards.

"I've often thought about Thorpe and his punting," once said Greasy Neale, player and coach from the pioneer days. "He had to kick that balloon-shaped ball. With the pointed, narrow-shaped ball of today, he would have been able to punt from one goal line to the other. I never saw a kicker with his leg drive."

He had it for field-goal kicking, too. When he was old and fat, the Giants sometimes capitalized on the magic of his name by bringing him to the Polo Grounds to kick field goals between halves. The big Indian would stand at midfield, kick a ball between one set of goalposts, and then turn around and do the same toward the opposite end of the field.

Don't underestimate the expression, "the magic of his name." It was Thorpe with the Canton Bulldogs in 1915 who got pro ball onto the launching pad for its eventual shot into orbit. As the greatest and best adver-

Hall of Fame
Jim Thorpe (5th from left, back row) led Oorang Indians of NFL in 1922. Sponsored by Oorang Kennels of Marion, Ohio, team had Airedale as its mascot. His Indians' teammates had such colorful names as Wrinkle Meat, Little Twig, Eagle Feather, Bear Behind, Long Time Sleep and Running Deer.

16

tised player in the country, he gave the still foundering pro football enterprise a stability that he alone could have supplied.

If his fame had come on college gridirons, what did it really matter? The pro people were gratefully picking up whatever crumbs they could find in those days and were more than half a century away from being able to sneer condescendingly at their campus inferiors.

There are so many colleges playing so many sports in so many areas nowadays that it becomes a gigantic blur. In Thorpe's day, however, it was simple and clearcut. The Northeastern segment of the United States dominated the entire sports front. It had Yale, Harvard, Princeton, Army, Navy, and some valiant independents. The national champion usually was to be found among them.

The champion of 1910 had been Harvard and it is to be doubted that few of the lordly Cantabs had even heard of one 1911 foe, Carlisle Institute. It was a little Indian school in the Pennsylvania hills and actually wasn't much better than a high school in quality. But it had a genius for a coach, Glenn Scobie ("Pop") Warner.

Being an arch manipulator, Pop arranged a game with Harvard. The Crimson was three-deep in manpower under the brilliant Percy Haughton. Carlisle wasn't deep in anything—except Jim Thorpe. There were only 16 Indians on the squad, some of them no heavier than 170 pounds.

The Crimson horde swept easily for a touchdown. Into action moved the mighty Sac and Fox. He pounded into scoring territory and kicked a 23-yard field goal. He booted a 45-yarder and a 37-yarder. To the vast astonishment of the pro-Harvard gathering at Cambridge, little Carlisle led at the half, 9 to 6.

The Harvards were indignant when play resumed. In cold fury the Crimson jerseys returned to the fray and contemptuously brushed aside the upstarts who were bedeviling them. Quickly Harvard put together a touchdown and field goal for a seemingly safe lead of 15–9. Then Thorpe walked over to Gus Welch, the quarterback.

"Gimme the ball," he said. He made the demand nine times. On the ninth time he rocketed over the goal line for a touchdown. It was 15–15 and Harvard was willing to settle for the tie. Thorpe wasn't.

The Sac and Fox kept slashing and driving at the Harvard line as the game entered its closing minutes. He was a one-man gang. Then the desperate Crimson braced beyond midfield on the 43-yard line. It was fourth down and everyone in the ball park knew that the Indian surge had been blunted—except Thorpe.

"Set the ball up," ordered Big Jim of Welch, the quarterback. "I'll kick a field goal."

"From midfield?" asked Welch.

"Yes, from midfield," snarled the Sac and Fox.

His 50-yarder split the posts and won the game. It was his fourth field goal and he had scored every point in Carlisle's 18–15 victory.

Thorpe's football debut was against Penn and he was so green that he barely knew the signals. But the starting left halfback was injured and Pop Warner suddenly remembered the sight of Thorpe threading his way through tacklers in a practice scrimmage. He sent him in. It was instant disaster. He tumbled over his own blockers and went down ignominiously. He arose and looked downfield at the goal line 65 yards away. It was something he could recognize.

Rather than risk more entanglement, he let his interference go its way, while he went his. He left seven Penn tacklers strewn over the landscape as he spun 65 yards for a touchdown.

Hall of Fame

The famed backfield that put Carlisle Institute on the football map.
(From left): Pete Calac, Jim Thorpe, Joe Guyon and Guy Chamberlain.

"This is fun," said Jim. "Let me try it again." They let him try. He went 85 yards for a touchdown the next time.

In a game against Dickinson, a sturdy foe, the Carlisle center passed the ball over Thorpe's head in a punt situation. He recovered the ball in the back of the end zone and ran 110 yards for a touchdown. Against Lehigh, then a powerhouse, he intercepted a pass in the end zone and ripped 105 yards downfield with it for a touchdown.

One of his more notable exhibitions was against Army at West Point in 1912. He went through the vaunted Army line as if it were an open door to score the first touchdown. He added a touch of variety by completing six straight passes to Arcasa for another touchdown. He ran back a kickoff 90 yards through the entire cadet team and into the end zone. But Carlisle was guilty of a rules infraction and the kickoff had to be repeated. Thorpe also repeated. He ran that one back 95 yards for a touchdown. Army was routed, 27–6. In trying to tackle Thorpe, one cadet was so severely injured that he never played football again. But he did rather well in other spheres of activity. His name was Dwight David Eisenhower.

Jim Thorpe was the son of Hiram Thorpe, whose parents had been an Irish adventurer and an Indian woman. Hiram also married an Indian, Charlotte View, the granddaughter of Chief Black Hawk, greatest of all Sac and Fox warrior chieftains. She was three-quarters Indian and one-quarter French. So Jim's ancestral strain was slightly mixed, since he was five-eighths Indian, one-quarter Irish and one-eighth French.

"It makes me an American Airedale of sorts," he once said whimsically. He was born in Oklahoma on May 28, 1888, and was therefore still in his athletic prime when he brought his tremendous, matchless prestige into professional football with the Canton Bulldogs in 1915. Six years before the formation of the National Football League, the play-for-pay operatives were scrounging and scraping for attention. There wasn't a better attention-getter in the country than Jim Thorpe.

The only criticism Pop Warner had ever leveled at his Indian marvel was that Thorpe didn't always put out 100 per cent of himself for every minute of every game. He would get moody and lose concentration. That would reduce him to being slightly less than superman.

The hottest rivalry in pro ball in those early years was between the Canton Bulldogs and Massillon Tigers, unfriendly neighbors. They played a scoreless tie. Thorpe was dull, uninspired, and uninterested. But when the return match came around, he was at an emotional peak. Massillon had loaded up with the most famous forward-passing combination of that era, Gus Dorais and Knute Rockne of Notre Dame. They also helped hypo the gate.

The Indian was magnificent. A defensive whirlwind, he put a smothering blanket on the Dorais-Rockne passing combination. They did not complete a pass. The Canton Bulldogs won, 28–0. Thorpe scored every point.

No man in the history of football ever saw more players than the saintly Amos Alonzo Stagg. On his 100th birthday he submitted to interviews and was asked about the Indian.

"Football will never see another as great as Jim Thorpe," said the Grand Old Man of the gridiron.

"Thorpe was the theoretical super-player in flesh and blood," said Percy Haughton of Harvard.

"You, sir, are the greatest athlete in the world," said King Gustaf V of Sweden.

Any of them would serve neatly as Jim Thorpe's epitaph.

Sweeps right end against New York Giants for good gain in 1930 contest at Polo Grounds.

Red Grange

Red Grange

by Joseph Durso

UPI
Spectacular runner at Illinois U., he follows blocker downfield.

In the days before television and moon landings, the dramatic peaks of American life were often supplied by working heroes on working stages. Babe Ruth packing his gear and heading for New York with a baseball bat. John McGraw in the Polo Grounds as king of a hill that Ruth would soon climb. Thomas A. Edison in his laboratory at Menlo Park, New Jersey. Ethel and John Barrymore at the Empire Theatre. Bill Tilden at Forest Hills. And, in 1921, Jack Dempsey and Georges Carpentier drawing the first million-dollar gate at a place called Boyle's Thirty Acres in New Jersey.

It was a time of "reparations payments," suffragism, Prohibition, bootleggers, rum courts and great race horses like Man O' War who broke the track record or world record in eight of his eleven starts

as a three-year-old. It was also a time when professional football began to join the stampede, even though it customarily resembled a stampede itself. But starting with a company team that played in a grassy park behind Hagemeister's Brewery in Green Bay, Wisconsin, football established a beachhead on the scene that eventually changed the scene itself.

Football's beachhead was a precarious one, though, because the 11-man gangs who played it then usually lacked the "star quality" of other entertainment. It was a rough, grudging sport that gave little running room—or operating room—to virtuoso performers.

"We played for the love of the game," Curly Lambeau recalled. "We agreed to split any money we got and each man was to pay his own doctor's bills."

When they ended their first season, the 21 pioneers who had put the Green Bay Packers on the map indeed split the money and pocketed $16.75 apiece. For other pioneers, the rewards were just as meager. A ceramic engineer from the University of Illinois named George Halas organized a similar team, Staley's Bears, that lost only two of 14 games in 1920. They switched their operations to Chicago the next year and, for their season's labors, lost $71.63.

What they needed was some kind of organization to rescue all the early teams from the sandlots, plus some "names" to rescue them from the poorhouse. They got the organization after a caucus in Canton, Ohio, and for a membership fee of $100 they opened the doors of the American Professional Football Association to teams like the Canton Bulldogs, the Massilon Tigers and the Rochester Kodaks. A short time later, in 1921, they reduced the fee to $50 and changed the name to the National Football League. But they still urgently needed money and the magic "name" that would produce it.

They finally got both in November, 1925, after three franchises had failed in Cleveland and three in Detroit, with 20 teams still scraping out an existence from Providence to Kansas City. The provider was an Illinois senior named Harold E. ("Red") Grange, and he began to provide the star quality right after his final college game.

Red Grange: born in Forksville, Pennsylvania, on June 13, 1903; the son of a lumberjack; a boy who, at the age of 8, was ordered to abandon all forms of strenuous exercise because of a heart murmur. But six years later, a physician at Wheaton High School in Illinois found no trace of the heart murmur and Grange became a 138-pound member of the freshman football team.

After that, he dealt strictly in improbable statistics. As a freshman, he played right

24

UPI
Red Grange is hemmed in by U. of Chicago players as Harry Thomas (2) tries to tackle the Illini all-American in muddy 1924 battle.

end, caught no passes and handled the ball once—when he took the kickoff in the final game and ran 70 yards for a touchdown. As a sophomore, he was shifted to halfback: 15 touchdowns, nine extra points, and an overall total of 99. As a junior, after an ice truck rolled over his left knee: 36 touchdowns, 39 conversions, and 255 points. And as a senior: 23 touchdowns, 34 conversions, and 172 points.

He did it mainly by fancy footwork, which he also used in baseball, basketball and track, often running the 100- and 200-yard dashes and the hurdles in the same meet. Then, after a mild overture (without any particular inducement) from the University of Michigan, he headed for Illinois. He made the choice because it was the least expensive school on his horizon, because a neighbor named George Dawson played there, and because he once had met Bob Zuppke, the football coach at Illinois, who said:

"If you come here to school, I believe you'll stand a good chance of making our football team."

He made it, all right. He weighed only 166 pounds and stood just under six feet, but he still had that fancy footwork and speed—and a 240-pound fullback named Earl Britton who for the next four years ran interference for the well-mannered blond ball-carrier from Wheaton. He also had a big afternoon against the varsity in the annual full-dress mismatch—scoring two touchdowns, one on a 60-yard punt return, though the freshmen finished on the shy end of the 21–19 score.

Then, another summer of delivering ice on the truck, and Grange was a sophomore halfback on Zuppke's varsity, opening the season against Nebraska. After one quarter,

25

he was scolded by Zuppke for "tipping off" the plays by leaning, and he confessed: "I'm so excited out there that I don't know where they're going myself." But after four quarters, he had figured it out well enough to run for three touchdowns while the Illini barreled to a 24–7 victory.

"It was a spectacular piece of work," observed Walter Eckersall, the old Chicago hero, "the sort expected of a player with the speed of the former Wheaton star, who has all the earmarks of developing into a wonderful player."

Wonderful, indeed. Against Northwestern, the following week, he went 90 yards for a touchdown during a 29–0 cruise. Against Butler, he scored two quick ones and then watched from the sidelines while Illinois won by 21–7. Against Iowa, Britton kicked a 53-yard field goal that stood up until the fourth period, when Iowa broke through for a touchdown. But the sophomores matured fast, with Britton passing four times to Grange, who finally won the game on a two-yard plunge.

Next came Amos Alonzo Stagg and his University of Chicago team, appearing in Champaign for the opening of the new $2,000,000 Illinois stadium and determined to isolate Grange by controlling the ball. They did control it, too, limiting Grange to only 17 carries, but he gained 173 yards and scored the only touchdown of the game. Against Wisconsin the next week, he again scored the only touchdown, and Britton kicked a 33-yard field goal for a 10–0 victory.

Two games to go: a breather against Mississippi A&M, which Grange sat out, and a toughie against Ohio State, which he iced with a 34-yard touchdown run in the final period. Sophomore totals: 12 touchdowns, unbeaten season, all-American rating.

Not only that, but Illinois shared the conference championship with Fielding Yost's Michigan team. The two schools had not played each other that year, but they did have a date the following year, and by then the scouting report on the 20-year-old "Galloping Ghost" read like this:

"The Illinois offense is built around Red Grange and Earl Britton. Grange carries the ball practically 75 per cent of the time on short and wide end runs, off-tackle and cutbacks. His end running attacks are successful, due to two things: one, a wonderful superman who uses all the tricks of a good halfback's stock in trade; and two, some extremely effective interference and blocking. In the Wisconsin game, his showing simply astounded the scouts, for his runs were only stopped by the Wisconsin team's forcing him out of bounds, and none of them were for less than 11 yards."

The date was October 18, 1924. The place was Memorial Stadium in Champaign. The crowd numbered 67,000. At stake was supremacy between the two undefeated western powers. The favorite: Michigan.

"Mr. Grange will be a carefully watched man every time he takes the ball," Coach Yost predicted. "There will be just about eleven clean, hard Michigan tacklers headed for him at the same time."

There were, too, and they headed for him as he cradled the opening kickoff on the 5-yard line. But few laid hands on him as he sprinted 95 yards to fire the opening shot in an historic duel.

A few minutes later, Illinois got the ball again and this time Grange circled left end for 67 yards and another touchdown. Then, an exchange of punts, and Grange exploded 56 yards for No. 3. And finally, another exchange and the identical play, 45 yards for another touchdown. Twelve minutes had elapsed and Grange had crossed one of the best-defended goal lines in America four times, had gained 303 yards, and still had 48 minutes to go.

Zuppke, rising to the occasion, let him play all but two or three of those remaining minutes, and Grange obliged by adding a fifth touchdown late in the game and passing for another. The final score was 39–14. Grange's final total was 402 yards on 21 carries for five TD's, plus six completed passes for 78 yards and another touchdown.

After that, they rested the Ghost against Depauw, then watched him score twice in the first quarter against Iowa. Then came the roughest test of his undergraduate days against Stagg and Chicago—"possession ball" so relentlessly executed that Illinois got the ball for only one play in the first period. By then, Chicago was seven points in front and went 14 points up as the second period began, before Grange gained 20 yards rushing and 47 more passing en route to Illinois's first score.

Things were threatening to get out of hand at 21–7 when Britton and Grange revived again. Grange gained 40 yards on runs, 44 more on passes and scored again to make it 21–14. Then, in the third quarter, he flashed 80 yards for a 21-all tie.

It was a monumental struggle and it depleted Illinois for the rest of the season, though Grange had gained 300 yards on the ground and 150 more in the air. In the next game, they were taken by Minnesota, 20–7, with Red scoring from the 10-yard line. And in the finale, he sat with a wrenched shoulder while Ohio State edged out a 7–0 victory. But the season's marks were still farfetched: 1,164 yards gained on the ground in six starts, 534 gained by passing, and 13 touchdowns.

By 1925, Grange was a senior surrounded by a fading team. He managed only six touchdowns that season, but three of them were scored against undefeated Pennsylvania in the snow before 65,000 customers in Franklin Field. Penn had been a five-touchdown favorite and Illinois had

Hall of Fame
Grange and C. C. ("Cash-and-Carry") Pyle, who organized epic barnstorming trip in 1925.

won only one of its four previous games, but the final score was 24–2, with Grange going for 363 yards, a performance that moved Damon Runyon to write:

"This man Red Grange is three or four men and a horse rolled into one. He is Jack Dempsey, Babe Ruth, Al Jolson, Paavo Nurmi and Man O' War."

He also was a one-man show who filled stadiums with people storming the gates to watch No. 77 in action, who received 50 letters a day from women alone, who once was locked inside his hotel room for safety while a substitute impersonated him in a parade, who scored 31 touchdowns and gained 4,280 yards as an undergraduate. Then he met a theater owner named C. C. Pyle—"Cash-and-Carry" Pyle—who shook hands and asked: "How would you like to make $100,000 or maybe a million?"

For Grange, who had just played three varsity seasons for nothing, that sounded reasonable enough and he agreed to a 50-50 split with Pyle. In turn, Pyle peddled him to George Halas and the Chicago Bears, who haggled for 26 hours in the Morrison Hotel in Chicago before settling for a two-thirds/one-third deal—two-thirds for Grange, one-third for the Bears. In effect, it meant that Grange, Pyle and the Bears each owned a third of the action. The "action" consisted of an exhibition schedule that Pyle had already drawn: seven games in 10 days, interspersed with the Bears' remaining league games, then three more starts in the week after that, then a one-week vacation, and finally an eight-game winter tour of Florida and California.

The whole scheme hinged on a "must"—Grange must play 30 minutes of every exhibition, a condition that created the National Football League and that physically devastated Red Grange. But the partnership began dramatically on Thanksgiving Day before a sellout crowd of 36,000 in Wrigley Field: the Bears against the Chicago Cardinals. It was the largest crowd that had ever watched a pro football game, and it did not seem too disappointed when the Cards kicked the ball away from Grange and he failed to cross anybody's goal line in a scoreless tie.

Grange wasn't too disappointed, either, because he pocketed his first paycheck afterward and it totaled $50,000. A week later, they drew 70,000 fans in New York, where Tim Mara had been something like $200,000 in the red with a limping franchise. Incredibly, the day before, they had played in Philadelphia before 40,000 persons in a driving rainstorm in Shibe Park, and in two other games that week before 36,000 combined in St. Louis and Frankford.

The Galloping Ghost, now galloping to the bank as well as to the goal line, scored

UPI
Grange runs past fallen Wilson Wildcat player at Yankee Stadium when he starred for New York Yankees of the new American League in 1926.

four touchdowns in St. Louis, two in Philadelphia and another in New York, where his check weighed $40,000. Then the caravan headed for Washington on Tuesday, Boston on Wednesday, Pittsburgh on Thursday, Detroit on Saturday, and back to Chicago on Sunday. The star of the cast reinjured a bad shoulder in Pittsburgh, had to sit out the game in Detroit, and saw $20,000 in tickets refunded.

After that, they dragged into Coral Gables, Florida, where seats went for $19.80 apiece, and then to Tampa, New Orleans, Los Angeles, San Francisco, Seattle, and Portland. They played 19 games in five weeks. Grange frequently broke down in exhaustion, but he netted close to $200,000, and put the NFL in business. He even started his own league when the Bears resisted a demand for a one-third share of the club.

When the Grange-Pyle league folded, the entrepreneurs neatly shifted to the NFL and New York as the Yankees. But time and all those hard knocks had taken their toll, and a severe knee injury sidelined the Ghost in 1927. Vaudeville, a movie or two, the Depression—all served to bury the legend, until he fired a few parting shots in the early 1930's with the Bears.

But in his trail, he left an industry headed for preeminence on the sporting scene, as well as the echoes of the huge crowds roaring, as No. 77 stepped toward the sideline before cutting back against the grain.

"All Grange can do is run," the *Michigan Daily* had said with some peevishness during the glory years. To which his old coach, Bob Zuppke, replied: "All Galli-Curci [the famed operatic coloratura soprano] can do is sing."

"When Pavlova danced," Zuppke reflected on another occasion, putting the legend into perspective, "nobody tried to trip her. When Grange ran, eleven men

were trying to stop him, and the job he did avoiding them was just as beautiful."

And another time, when the Michigan team years later was being psyched by the presence of Tommy Harmon, the Illinois team was being psyched by Zuppke, who observed from long memory: "Harmon is a great back, but Grange's ghost is better."

29

UPI

Keeps driving despite Giants' defender on his back as Mel Hein (7) reaches out to stop him in 1934 NFL championship game and Bo Molenda (23) and Ed Danowski (22) rush over to assist.

Bronko Nagurski

Bronko Nagurski
by Lud Duroska

Bear Bryant, the veteran college coach, is reputed to have said it first:

"Football is not a contact sport. Dancing is. Football is a *hitting* sport."

And no player ever lived up to that definition more wholeheartedly than Bronko Nagurski of the Chicago Bears, the most feared fullback of his time. There never was a harder hitter than the Bronk—and not just as a runner. He loved to hit—whether he was carrying the ball, blocking, or tackling—and his opponents had the scars to show for it.

One was Steve Owen, an immense tackle for the New York Giants, who used to say: "See these bumps on my head? I got most of them from trying to stop the Bronk. The others came from trying to tackle the old Indian, Jim Thorpe."

And Nagurski had other impressive football qualities, too.

UPI
Nagurski's powerful legs pull him out of Philadelphia Eagles' grasp.

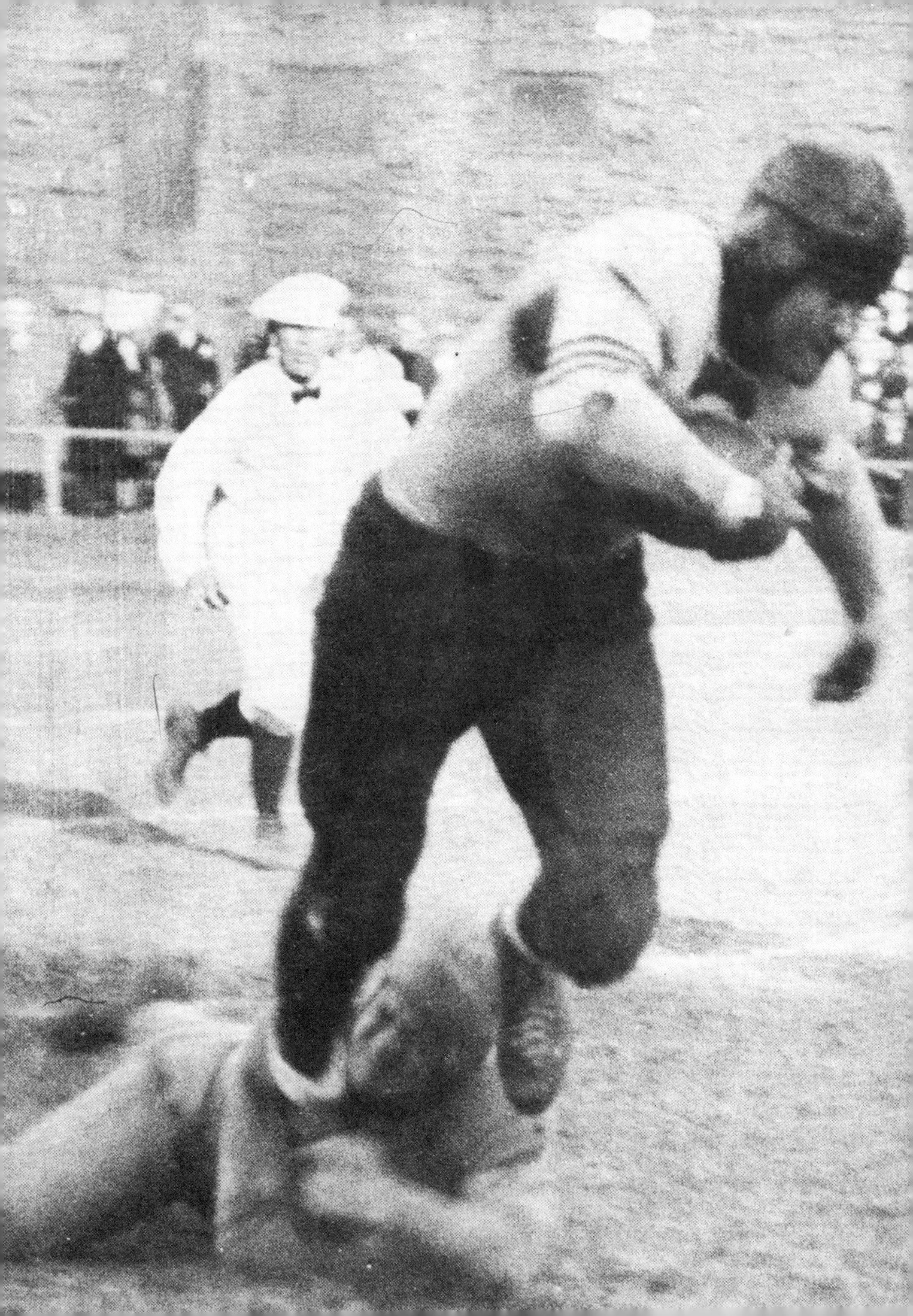

Can you imagine a player so *good* that he was picked as an all-American at two positions in the same season? Or a player so *strong* that he once scored the winning touchdown with six tacklers on his back? Or a player so *tough* that a NFL coach said the only sure way to stop him is to shoot him before he leaves the locker room?

That was Bronko Nagurski, and it's no wonder he was described as "the most devastating one-man thundering herd ever seen in football."

When he charged into a would-be tackler, he possessed all the single-minded purpose and irresistible force of a bowling ball crashing into the pins. He ran low to the ground, and he ran over and through the defenders. It was said he was the only back who provided his own interference.

The other team had to gang up on him, partly for reasons of self-preservation. The practical way to defense the Bronk was called the one-two-three system. The first tackler tried to slow him down, the second to bring him down, and the third to make certain he stayed down.

The stories abound on his unquenchable desire to keep driving, driving toward the end zone. Perhaps the most famous tale concerns his epic run against Portsmouth when he was a second-year pro with the Bears. The Bronk burst through center, sent two linebackers reeling backward, blasted over the defensive halfback, straight-armed the safetyman, and crashed into a goal post. When he came to, he supposedly said: "That last guy hit me awfully hard."

Even in scrimmages, the Bronk was gung-ho, and his teammates disliked tackling him. Red Grange recalled: "When he hit you, it was like getting an electric shock. And if you hit him above the ankles, you could get killed."

On defense, Nagurski was just as ferocious. His favorite tackling maneuver was a shattering cross-body block that slammed the runner to the ground and caused more than a few fumbles.

In height and weight, Bronko was no giant by comparison with today's pro football performers. He stood 6-feet-2 inches tall and weighed no more than 230 pounds at the peak of his career. But how he was built! Shoulders the width of a door, a bull neck, a massive chest, and arms and legs bulging with muscle.

It makes more understandable the reason he earned the distinction—never accorded to another player—of all-American honors at two positions simultaneously. After his senior year at the University of Minnesota, many selectors placed him at fullback, where he had played most of the time that season. But others, wanting to include Purdue's excellent fullback, Ralph Welch, simply switched Nagurski to tackle, where he had already been an all-American. And one writer showed his high regard for Bronko by naming only nine players and putting him at both tackle and fullback.

As a pro, he was an instant star with the Bears in 1930. The Chicago club had been near the bottom of the league the year before, but with the Bronk the Bears improved enough to finish in third place. By 1932 they were in the NFL championship game, and again in 1933 and in 1934. He played in his fourth title contest in 1937 and then retired. Or so he thought.

During the World War II manpower shortage, he answered an SOS from the Bears. He returned to action in 1943 at the age of 35, this time as a tackle, but he had a final fling at fullback in a crucial late-season game. And then he helped win another NFL crown for Chicago, scoring a touchdown in the title playoff against the Washington Redskins. It was a fine way to end a career.

* * *

Nature played its part in molding this remarkably rugged athlete. He was a true son of the Northland, that part of Minnesota near the Canadian border where the winters are long and hard, full of ice and snow, and below-zero temperatures are as common as sunshine in Miami. Bronko himself once observed: "Actually, we don't have any summer up here. We just have a season in the middle of the year when the sledding is poor."

His parents were immigrants from the Ukraine. They first settled in the small town of Rainy River in the Province of Ontario, where a son was born on November 3, 1908, and christened Bronislau Nagurski. He was four years old when the family moved across the border to International Falls, Minnesota, and his father opened a grocery store. He grew to manhood in International Falls, returned there after every football season, and continued to make it his home after his playing days were over.

Legend has it that he received the nickname of Bronko—and how appropriate a name it proved to be!—when his mother brought him to school for the first time. She had difficulty, with her heavy accent, in making the teacher understand that his first name was Bronislau. So the teacher called him Bronko.

Hall of Fame
Bronko Nagurski fakes out one potential tackler as he shifts into high gear.

Nagurski was also an above-average passer.

Fame eluded him as a high school player—for good reason. Unbelievable as it may sound, his team failed to win a game in his two seasons on the squad. He was an unknown when he arrived on the Minnesota campus in the fall of 1926. But it didn't take long for Coach Doc Spears to notice him at practice in the midst of the more heralded prospects.

The story is told that Spears had worked out a special off-tackle play he wanted the varsity to spring on Michigan in the opening game. The Gophers' coach was certain it would result in a long gain because he had a standout fullback in Herb Joesting.

Spears tried out the play against the freshman team. But, much to his chagrin, every time Joesting passed the scrimmage line and seemed in the open, Nagurski appeared, plugging up the hole and stopping Joesting for no gain.

Still convinced the play had merit, Spears decided to let the freshmen run it against the varsity. Bronko was given the ball. He broke into the clear and would have scored if it had been a regular game. To make sure that wasn't a fluke, Spears had the play run over again, and again Bronko raced far downfield. The Minnesota coach could only conclude that the play was okay, but whether it worked or not depended on whether Nagurski was on the defense or the offense.

Bronko's versatility was amply demonstrated during his college career—he was put where he was needed most. As a freshman, he was stationed at end. In his sophomore year, he was shifted to tackle because the Gophers' varsity was plentifully supplied with good ends and had Joesting, who was to make all-American that season, at fullback.

Mighty Notre Dame and its famed coach, Knute Rockne, soon learned about this fierce competitor, for he was instrumental in spoiling one of their most cherished records: a Rockne team had never been defeated or tied on its home field.

The Fighting Irish were ahead, 7–0, and moving toward another touchdown when the tide was suddenly turned. As the Notre Dame back pounded into the line, Nagurski met him head-on in a violent collision. The ball was jarred loose and Bronko fell on the fumble. The elated Gophers took over and marched for the tying score. The game ended in a 7–7 tie, putting the first blot on Rockne's amazing home record.

In his junior and senior years Bronko made the headlines as the rampaging fullback on offense and the unyielding tackle

36

on defense. But sometimes he had to be deployed elsewhere in emergency situations. Minnesota was badly crippled in a game against Iowa when several Gopher regulars were forced to the sidelines with injuries. Before the afternoon was over, he played end, tackle, guard, halfback, and fullback. Despite Bronko's yeoman efforts, the Gophers lost. But Minnesota was a power in the Big Ten with the Bronk on its side and every season with him in uniform was a winning one.

After Bronko's collegiate exploits, George Halas was eager to sign him for the Bears. The Chicago owner offered him $3,500. Nagurski asked for $6,500, and they compromised at $5,000. If the low figures are shocking, it must be remembered that pro football was still struggling for survival and his salary was typical of its day. Of course, it's also true that Halas was not known as a spendthrift. "We used to say that he tossed nickles around like they were manhole covers," Bronko commented years later.

And $5,000 a year was the most he ever got as a pro. The depression arrived by the next season, and Nagurski had to take a cut in pay in 1931, along with every other wage-earner in the country. Even though he was a star, it took several seasons, in fact, before he was paid $5,000 again.

UPI
Charges ahead as Giants' Ed Danowski slips and Bo Molenda (23), Ray Flaherty (1) and Cecil ("Tex") Irvin (29) close in on him during 1934 title game.

His reputation preceded him into the NFL, and some pros were curious to find out if the Bronk was as strong and tough as his press clippings trumpeted. This curiosity led to a memorable incident in his second game as a pro rookie, and it involved the best lineman in the league, Cal Hubbard of the Green Bay Packers.

Hubbard, a 270-pound tackle who later became a well-known baseball umpire, was anxious to test Nagurski. Early in the game the Bears went into punt formation with Bronko as the deep blocker. Hubbard made an unusual request of the opposing Bears' tackle.

"I promise you I won't block the kick," Hubbard said, "but you'd do me a favor if you'd step aside and let me get a clean shot at Nagurski."

The Bears' tackle obliged, and Hubbard roared into the backfield straight for Bronko. They met and Hubbard went sailing backward. When he got up, he shook his head and said to the Bears' tackle, "Please don't do me any more favors. Now I know."

And the rest of the NFL was not long in finding out, either.

Squads of 18 players were common in that era that meant many were on the field for all 60 minutes of the game, which was all right with the Bronk. He always wanted to be in the thick of the action.

After the modern era with its platoons and specialists arrived, Nagurski was asked what he thought about the sport.

"I guess it's a better game," he said, "but if I was playing now, I wouldn't be able to play all the positions I did in my day.

"And if I had to stick with one position, I'm not even sure I would want to be the fullback. I think what I would like to play would be middle linebacker. I used to play what we called a roving center and I liked that. I guess I liked defense better than offense. And blocking better than running."

Ironic words from the man whose bruising running feats still remain the gauge by which all other fullbacks are measured.

Complete statistics, unfortunately, were not kept in the NFL in 1930 and 1931, his first two seasons, so there's some question as to exactly how much yardage Nagurski bulldozed his way to. The generally agreed-upon figures are 4,031 yards in 872 carries for an average of 4.6 yards. They will do.

There have been faster fullbacks and slicker ones, but only the incomparable Jim Brown is rated close to Nagurski for sheer hitting power. And his all-round ability puts the Bronk in a class by himself. Old-timers have said eleven Nagurskis could have beaten eleven Granges, or eleven Thorpes, or eleven anyone-else, for that matter.

When pro football's Hall of Fame was becoming a reality in Canton, Ohio, and the panel of judges assembled, they pondered, debated, and finally settled on 17 they felt were worthy of the honor of being in the first group to be enshrined. Naturally, one was Bronislau ("Bronko") Nagurski.

UPI
Two Giants (Mel Hein on left) attempt to bulldoze Nagurski to the ground.

39

UPI
Shows grim determination as he starts on 71-yard touchdown run against Brooklyn Dodgers in 1948 game.

Steve Van Buren

Steve Van Buren

by Murray Chass

To say Steve Van Buren was a bruising, punishing runner is like saying the Los Angeles freeways have traffic jams.

Jack Ferrante, a Philadelphia Eagles' teammate, once learned unintentionally how bruising Van Buren was. During a game, Van Buren cut sharper than usual in trying to avoid a charging tackler and smashed into Ferrante, Philadelphia's right end. As Ferrante lay on the ground, a look of pain spreading over his face, a member of the opposing team walked by.

"Hurts, doesn't it?" the player said. "Now you know how we feel when we try to tackle him."

Dick Wildung, a capable Green Bay Packer linebacker, also learned—the hard way. Wildung had stopped Van Buren on successive plays, a feat that perhaps understandably gave him the right to boast. But he boasted to the wrong fellow.

Hall of Fame
Leaps out of Washington Redskin's arms.

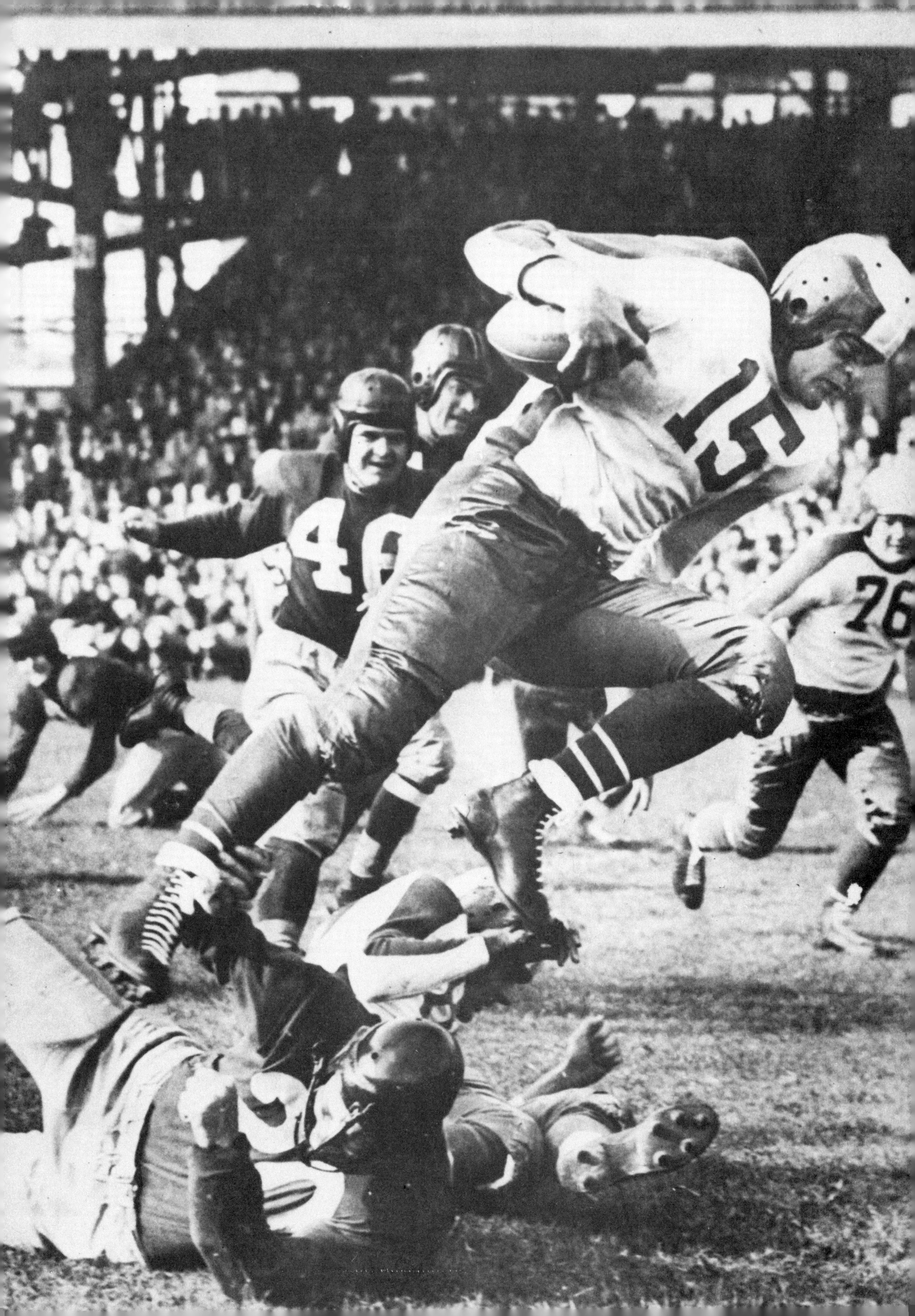

"You better tell your quarterback to stop calling that play," the linebacker brashly told Van Buren, "or I'm gonna kill you right in front of all these people."

So Van Buren returned to the huddle, barked to the quarterback, "Gimme the ball," and a moment later took the football and bowled over Wildung, leaving him sprawled on the ground, wondering whether he had been hit by a truck or a bus.

And then there was the Pittsburgh Steeler lineman who during a game was acting as if Van Buren was his personal battering board. A knee here, an elbow there, a finger in this eye, a thumb in that one. After a particularly aggravating poke, Van Buren went to Allie Sherman, the Eagles' reserve quarterback, and said, "On the next play, you give me the ball."

Van Buren mentioned the number of the play and before the huddle broke, he looked at the two linemen who on that play were supposed to double-team the offending Steeler. "You two guys get out of the way," he said. "I want to take this guy myself."

The players started to object, but Van Buren silenced them. Then Sherman faked a handoff to the fullback and gave the ball to Van Buren.

"When I turned around," Sherman recalled, "Steve had hit the guy, run right through him, and was off to a touchdown. The guy was lying there, stretched on the ground. He was out cold."

That Steve Van Buren should grow up to be a 6-foot-1-inch, 208-pound human bulldozer was a completely unexpected development to anyone who knew him as a 125-pound, 15-year-old high school student. It was just as unexpected that a youngster born in a tiny banana port in Honduras should become interested in football to the point of becoming one of the greatest backs in pro football history.

Born to an American fruit inspector and his Spanish wife in 1920, Steve came to the

UPI
Steve Van Buren turns the corner against Dodgers.

United States at the age of 10. His parents had died and he went to New Orleans to live with his grandparents.

"In Honduras I was too young to play much except simple running games and we'd never heard of football," Van Buren related. "But when I was 15 and in high school, I used to watch the other boys play football. It seemed like a good game, so I went out for the team. But I weighed only 125 pounds, and all the coach would let me do was run up and down the field with the other boys. When it came to playing football, he told me to forget about it. He was afraid I'd get hurt."

44

It was to be two years and 30 pounds later before young Steve tried football again, because after his first year in school, he dropped out and started working in an iron foundry.

"It was hard work, but I liked it and it built me up," he conceded.

Eventually, though, he decided to return to school, and this time when he went out for the football team he weighed 155 pounds. But while making him a member of the team, the coach placed him at end, even though he wanted to run with the ball.

He had similar problems in college at Louisiana State University. He finally made it to the backfield, but his coach, Bernie Moore, made him the blocking back. Moore already had a boy he thought was a good halfback. His name was Alvin Dark, and he later proved to be a much better shortstop with a long career in the major leagues.

But before the 1943 season, Dark went into military service and LSU was left without a runner. That's when Van Buren finally reached the position he had wanted to play since he was 15 years old. In his final year at LSU, Van Buren gained the second most yardage and scored the second highest number of points in the country, even though injuries limited his season to 6½ games. He returned in time for the Orange Bowl against Texas A&M and capped his year by running 35 and 55 yards for touchdowns and scoring a third on a pass in LSU's victory.

Based on the season Van Buren had, Moore recommended to the Eagles that they draft him No. 1, and they did. It was a particularly wise choice. While many of the top players had entered the service, Van Buren couldn't because of a chronic eye ailment.

After having his appendix out and arriving at the Eagles' training camp wearing shoes but no socks (a familiar sight today, but not in 1944), Van Buren proceeded to display the fast, elusive and bruising form that was to make him a star at Philadelphia until injuries began to take their toll in 1950 and finally ended his career in 1952.

As a rookie, the youngster with the crinkly brown hair got to run the ball only 80 times, but his average of 5.5 yards a carry was the tipoff on what was to come.

Van Buren led the league in rushing in 1945 with 832 yards. And in 1947, he did something only one other player previously had done in NFL history: he reached the magic 1,000-yard plateau. In so doing, he broke Beattie Feathers' rushing record by

45

four yards with 1,008, but two years later, the Eagles' famous No. 15 ran even farther, amassing 1,146 yards and becoming the first runner ever to reach the 1,000 mark twice.

The period of 1947 through 1949 was particularly pleasing to the Eagles because they played in the NFL championship game each of those seasons, winning twice.

In the first, against the Chicago Cardinals in 1947, Van Buren was limited to 26 yards on 18 carries on a frozen Comiskey Park field. The Eagles lost, 28–21. In the other two title contests, though, Steve was directly responsible for Philadelphia's championships.

The 1948 game, also against the Cardinals, was played at Shibe Park, which along with the rest of Philadelphia was inundated with snow by a fierce blizzard the day of the game. Workmen removed much of it from the playing surface, but that didn't do much for the scoring potential of the two clubs.

Finally, late in the third quarter, Bucko Kilroy recovered a Cardinal fumble at the Chicago 17-yard line, and shortly afterward Van Buren burst through the Cardinal defense for a five-yard touchdown, the only one in the 7–0 game. Almost incredibly, Van Buren totaled 98 yards on 26 carries that day.

If that performance was brilliant, think of how the Los Angeles Rams reacted when they watched almost helplessly the following year as Van Buren ripped apart their defense on a field muddied by a pouring rain for a total of 196 yards on 31 carries, a record for a championship game that still stands.

It was little wonder that Earle ("Greasy") Neale, his coach, called Van Buren the best halfback he ever saw. "Steve is as fast and as elusive as Red Grange," Neale said, "but

Hall of Fame
Van Buren struggles through snow into the end zone in 4th quarter for game's only touchdown in 1948 championship contest with the Cardinals.

UPI
Pat West of Cleveland Rams uses flying tackle to halt Steve Van Buren.

he doesn't need a blocker like Grange did. He can run over tacklers like Bronko Nagurski."

Neale's complete confidence and belief in Van Buren was never displayed better than in a rebuke the coach administered to Allie Sherman. It came after the future New York Giants' head coach had given the ball to Joe Muha, the fullback, when the Eagles had the ball close to the goal line. Sherman had used Van Buren on first down from the four and then on third down for the touchdown, but Neale was still angry.

"What are you trying to do?" Neale barked at Sherman when he came off the field.

"We scored six points. Is that wrong?" Sherman retorted.

"Yes," replied Neale. "You didn't give the ball to Van every time."

"Well, I figured I'd fool them a little," the reserve quarterback explained. "I had four downs to do it in."

"Listen, and don't ever forget it," the coach said sternly, "when you got the ball on the four-yard line with four chances to score, I want Van to get the ball every time, understand?"

Neale's appreciation for Van Buren's talents wasn't reserved only for his ground-gaining talents. In those days, when players went both ways, Van Buren was a top-notch defensive player, as well.

47

UPI
Van Buren takes advantage of block and swerves to right against Boston Yankees.

"Sometimes he drove me nutty on defense," the coach related. "But he was one of the best defensive players in the league. I never saw anybody who so consistently could run two or three blockers away from the ball-carrier and bring him down. He just feinted them away or slipped around them and got his man. But sometimes, as a safetyman, he got up so close you would think he was backing up the line. I would keep yelling at him to get back. He always did, in time; with his speed he could start late and still make it. But I wish he hadn't done it so often. It was bad for my ticker."

Van Buren didn't do much for other coaches' tickers either. Besides breaking Beattie Feathers' single-season rushing record, he shattered Clark Hinkle's career rushing record of 3,860 yards early in his sixth season (Hinkle played ten years), and in 1945 he eclipsed Don Hutson's record of 17 touchdowns by scoring 18—15 by rushing, two on pass catches, and one on a kickoff return.

But it was a touchdown he scored in 1946 that prompted Gus Dorais, the coach of the Detroit Lions, who were the victims, to say it was the greatest run he ever saw.

On the 65-yard romp, Van Buren, who had been playing only sporadically because of a bad cold and a high temperature, zigged and zagged all over the field. Practically every Lion had a shot at him, and five times he was knocked down. But, as the rules permitted in that era, he quickly scrambled back to his feet each time and kept going until he reached the end zone.

In 1950 he broke a toe and some ribs, and he—and the Eagles, along with him—started declining.

After a mediocre 1951 season, Van Buren, however, was optimistic that he could make a strong comeback in 1952. He was only 31 years old and he conceivably had some good years remaining. However, in the first scrimmage of the Eagles' training camp that year, he ran into bad luck.

A rookie lineman who didn't know his assignment tried to look as if he knew what he was doing. He pulled out of the line and turned the wrong way. As a result, he met Van Buren coming the other way and struck him on the side of his knee. The ligaments and cartilage in the knee were badly torn, and the knee was placed in a cast.

If the immediate-surgery theory so prevalent today had been in practice then, perhaps Steve could have returned the following season, if not sooner. But he wore the cast for so long that by the time it was removed, the knee had calcified and was stiff.

Determined to play again, Van Buren took innumerable whirlpool treatments and ran hundreds and hundreds of sprints. But he had lost the ability to pivot, and in trying to regain it, he practiced so much that a spur developed on the inside of his big toe.

That was the final blow, one from which he couldn't recover. But even though he played only eight seasons, he held nine records when he retired—five career marks, three for season totals, and one for a single-game performance. All of his records, of course, resulted from his great rushing feats. Passing wasn't his game.

"The fellow who threw the first pass," Van Buren once said, "must have been all through as a football player—or just too tired that day to run with the ball."

Van Buren never was too tired to run with the ball; he made only the defensive players weary.

			RUSHES				RECEPTIONS			
Year	Team	G.	Att.	Yds.	Avg.	TDs	No.	Yds.	Avg.	TDs
1944	Phil.	9	80	444	5.6	5	0	0	0.0	0
1945	Phil.	10	143	832	5.8	15	10	123	12.3	2
1946	Phil.	9	116	529	4.6	5	6	75	12.5	0
1947	Phil.	12	217	1,008	4.6	13	9	79	8.8	0
1948	Phil.	11	201	945	4.7	10	10	96	9.6	0
1949	Phil.	12	263	1,146	4.4	11	4	88	22.0	1
1950	Phil.	10	188	629	3.3	4	2	34	17.0	0
1951	Phil.	10	112	327	2.9	6	4	28	7.0	0
Totals		83	1,320	5,860	4.4	69	45	523	11.6	3

	PUNT RETURNS				KICKOFF RETURNS				SCORING	
Year	No.	Yds.	Avg.	TDs	No.	Yds.	Avg.	TDs	TDs	Pts.
1944	15	230	15.3	1	8	266	33.2	1	7	42
1945	14	154	11.0	0	13	373	28.7	1	18	*110
1946	5	89	17.8	1	11	319	29.0	0	6	36
1947	0	0	0.0	0	13	382	29.4	1	14	84
1948	0	0	0.0	0	14	292	20.9	0	10	60
1949	0	0	0.0	0	12	288	24.0	0	12	72
1950	0	0	0.0	0	5	110	22.0	0	4	24
1951	0	0	0.0	0	0	0	0.0	0	6	36
Totals	34	473	13.9	2	76	2,030	26.7	3	77	464

* Scoring includes 2 extra points.

UPI

Stiff-arms Stan Wallace of Bears in 1954 game.

Hugh McElhenny

Hugh McElhenny
by Parton Keese

They called him "The King." Broken-field runner extraordinary, superb pass receiver, an artist at the draw play, he was possessed of blinding speed, and noted for his great change of pace and many moves —a fake, a sidestep, a pivot, and even a pirouette. All those gridiron-royal qualities put Hugh McElhenny among the world's outstanding running backs. He was voted into the Hall of Fame the first year he became eligible, and whenever professional football stars got together, he was the recipient of majestic tributes.

"There never was an open-field runner like McElhenny," Y. A. Tittle, his quarterback for many years, once said. "He was the finest running back I ever saw."

"I've always felt," remarked Sam Huff, then the widely acclaimed middle linebacker of the New York Giants, "that Eastern fans were cheated because they had so

Hall of Fame
Gets by foe with swivel-hip move.

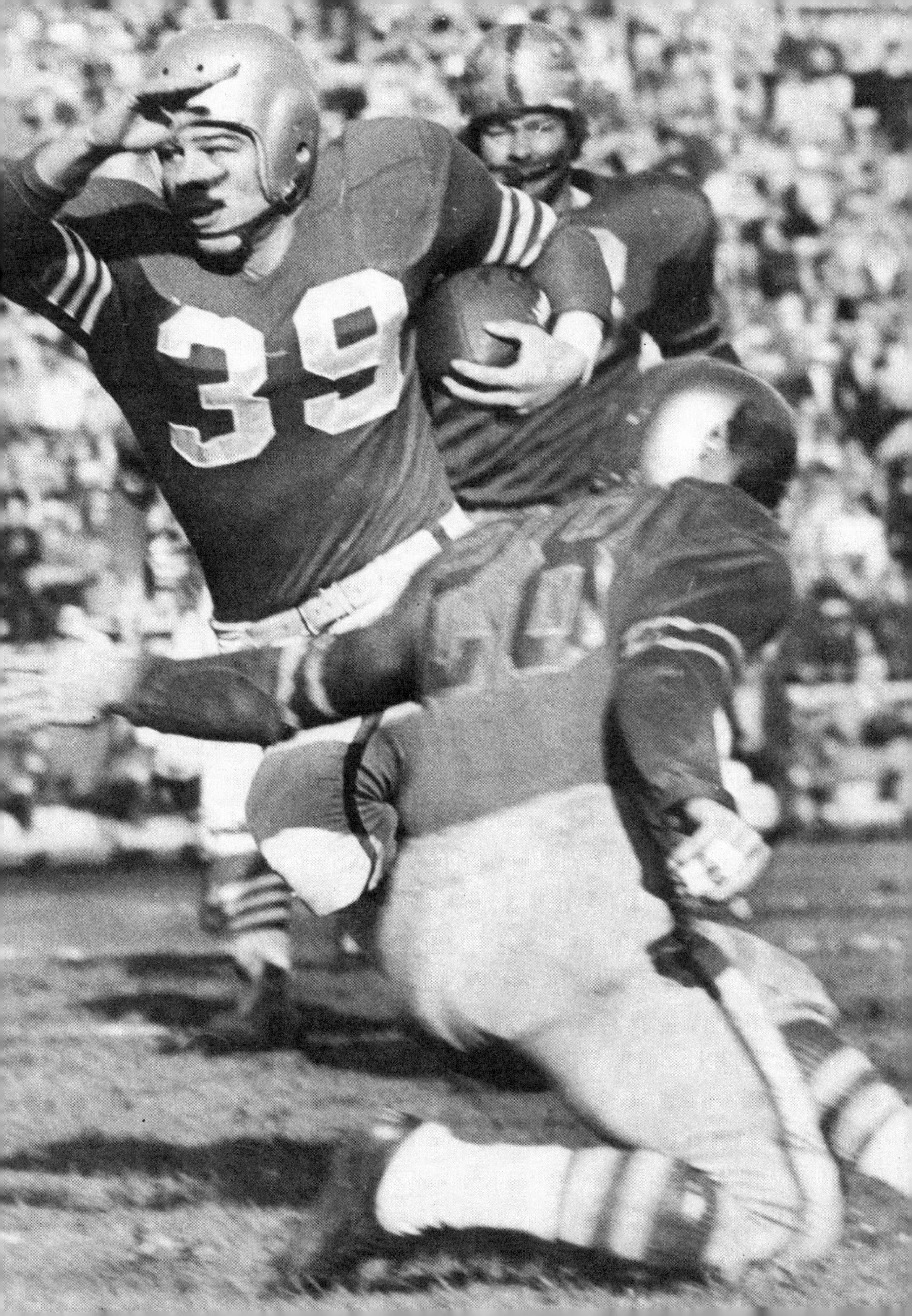

few opportunities to see The King in his prime. McElhenny played most of his 13 NFL seasons with the San Francisco 49ers. I saw too much of him. He gave me a heart attack every time he took the ball. I cannot remember ever tackling him solidly or throwing him for a loss."

McElhenny's coach at San Francisco, Buck Shaw, added this: "Hugh had more body rhythm and balance than any runner I've ever seen. We called him 'Slider' because of his unusual skill at sliding gracefully away from tacklers and leaving them grasping at space."

George Halas, the Chicago Bears' coach, felt that McElhenny changed the whole concept of drafting offensive backs. "Hugh convinced most of us that there wasn't much room in pro football for the 175-pound back. We not only needed them fast, but big and powerful. McElhenny was all three."

Bert Bell, Commissioner of professional football at that time, said flatly, "McElhenny is the best runner in the history of the National Football League."

Tommy Timkin, a football official for more than 25 years, went even further. He stated Hugh was the best runner of all time, college or pro.

McElhenny had another asset, fullback Joe Perry. It was Perry who shared a backfield spot on the 49ers and whose furious smashes up the middle complemented McElhenny's sweeps around the flanks. The defense had to pay so much attention to McElhenny, Perry became the league's leading ground-gainer one year with 1,018 yards. When they concentrated on Perry, McElhenny swept around end so often he also led the league with an average of 7 yards a carry.

Probably no two backs presented such a monumental problem to their opponents since Army's "Mr. Inside" and "Mr. Outside"—Doc Blanchard and Glenn Davis—raced up and down the field in the mid-40's. The pro version of the double onslaught had much in common, too. Both men were slightly taller than 6 feet, both ranged during the season between 198 and 205 pounds, both came from Compton, California, both could run 100 yards in 10 seconds or faster, and both drove the defenses crazy. While McElhenny was christened The King, Perry was dubbed The Little King.

When McElhenny was the subject of a story, it usually involved a great run and began, "Remember the game against. . . . ?" Y. A. Tittle's favorite was the 49ers' first game against the Los Angeles Rams in 1953. The Rams had drawn up what they considered a most detailed defensive plan, conceding Perry the short gains, but bottling up McElhenny by shooting two men at him from alternating positions at all times.

With three minutes to play, the Rams led, 30–28, and it looked as if the Rams' strategy had paid off. Los Angeles had allowed Perry the short gains, resulting in three touchdowns, but had held McElhenny to only 24 yards in 12 carries, with no completed passes and no points.

Badly confused and sitting on his own 20-yard line, Tittle, the 49er quarterback, asked Hugh if he felt he could get clear. Although the Rams had been sitting on his shoulders all day, he answered casually:

"You tell me where you're going to throw it. I'll be there."

Tittle decided on a screen pass to McElhenny, but the Rams weren't fooled. When Hugh caught the ball, four yards behind the scrimmage line, two tacklers came at him. He feinted one off his feet and tore loose from the other. Then he stiff-armed a third, hurdled a fourth and sprinted toward the sidelines between a fifth and sixth, both of whom grabbed a piece of him but couldn't hold on.

McElhenny in his best open-field form as Ed Meadows of Bears pursues him.

By the time McElhenny was finally cornered and knocked out of bounds on the Rams' 9-yard line, he had gained 71 yards. That set the stage for a field goal, which, just six seconds before the gun, wrapped up a 31–30 victory for San Francisco.

"McElhenny's run was the most incredible I've seen in football," exclaimed Ram coach Hampton Pool. "Our pictures showed that not one man in our defense was out of position. It was the only time he got away from us all day, but it was enough to beat us—that, together with Perry's three touchdowns. So what can you do to stop those guys?"

George Halas remembers a game in 1952, McElhenny's rookie season with the 49ers, when he picked up a football on the 6-yard line and ran 94 yards like a slithering snake through 11 Chicago Bears. He ran with such speed and deception that two Bears collided while reaching for him. Others fell to the ground in frustration, grasping for McElhenny and catching handfuls of air. With fluttering feet and a dancer's balance, McElhenny scored in his first official play as a pro.

At the sidelines Papa Bear Halas stared in wonder. "That's the damndest greatest run I've ever seen in football," he said. Later, in the dressing room, the San Francisco quarterback, Frankie Albert, said, "He's the king. McElhenny's the king of runners." The name stuck.

McElhenny always liked to start things off with a bang. In college, at the University of Washington, he electrified the fans the first time he got his hands on the ball, running 98 yards for a touchdown against Minnesota on the kickoff.

The first five passes thrown to McElhenny during his first exhibition season with the pros resulted in five touchdowns. In his rookie year he made the all-pro team, rushing for 684 yards in only 98 carries for a fantastic 14.1-yard average. He also scored 10 touchdowns, the most he ever achieved in any of his 13 seasons in the NFL.

For McElhenny himself, the first time he carried the ball in the pros is his favorite run. He was in an exhibition game against the Chicago Cardinals for exactly one play. He went 40 yards for a touchdown. "After that one," he said, "I thought I could make the pros. That's why I liked that one best."

Almost from the start, however, McElhenny was called a grandstander by some for the way he circled about in the end zone after scoring. Those people didn't understand, as McElhenny once explained:

"I got a kick every time I looked down and saw those end-zone stripes under my cleats. Then I circled in the end zone and looked back on the field to see if there were any penalty flags. I wasn't being flashy. Think of it this way:

"Every run of mine was caused by a defensive mistake. Sure, blockers are vital, but the blockers wouldn't be able to do their jobs if the defensive man made exactly the right moves at the right time. The defense then couldn't be moved out of position. So I looked back to make sure one of those mistakes wasn't an illegal one. Maybe I got into the end zone because somebody tripped somebody or clipped or held."

McElhenny's own linemen call him "a

UPI
Larry Benz (23) and Vince Costello (50) of Browns bear down on McElhenny.

thinking man's runner." Bob St. Clair, a 6-foot-8½-inch, 262-pound tackle with the 49ers, said, "Linemen seemed to get a certain lift when Hugh's number was called. So maybe we hooked just a little sharper and blocked just a little harder. We knew that if we did our job right on any of his plays, he could go for the big 6."

The most amazing fact about McElhenny may be that he could make it to a football field at all, much less the end zone. Born on December 31, 1928, of a wiry, 130-pound, 5-foot-4-inch father and a wispy Canadian mother, Hugh, when he was 11, stepped on a broken milk bottle, severing all the tendons in his right foot. He was out of school for a year, in bed for five months and on crutches for seven months. The doctors said he would never walk again.

"They said I'd wind up with a cane the rest of my life," McElhenny said. "But I began a series of exercises so that I could strengthen my foot. I kept working on it and when I was in my second year of high school, I made the football team. I still had problems, though. I wore a steel plate in the sole of my shoe and took shots before every game to help deaden the pain."

McElhenny went on to become a superstar in track and football. At George Washington High School in Los Angeles, he was clocked at 9.7 for the 100-yard dash and he set the world's interscholastic 120-yard hurdles record of 14 seconds flat. In his one season at Compton, which won 12 straight games, including the Little Rose Bowl match (the mythical national championship of junior colleges) McElhenny scored 23 touchdowns, 12 of them on runs of 30 yards and up.

Even with injuries, McElhenny frightened his opponents. In 1954, playing against the Chicago Bears, he suffered a

UPI
Playing for Vikings, McElhenny goes sailing after shoe-top tackle by a Packer.

McElhenny jumps high to elude Gary Lowe (left) and Dick LeBeau of Lions.

shoulder separation. San Francisco doctors said he would be out for the rest of the season. Just the same, the Rams, who were to meet the 49ers the following Sunday, spent the entire practice week installing a special defense against McElhenny—a man who wasn't even going to play. Explained ex-Ram coach Pool:

"Preparing for a team that lists McElhenny on the roster, you just can't take any chances."

Another time the 49ers invaded Wrigley Field to play the Bears. Halas, getting ready for the game, sat with his scout, listening to a report on the 49er offense. The scout droned on, illustrating with X's and O's. "O.K., O.K.," Halas finally interrupted. "Never mind that. Just tell me, where's McElhenny?"

Hugh gained 4,288 yards rushing with San Francisco in nine years, and in three of those years his total offense figures were over 1,000. He was a unanimous all-Pro in 1952 and 1953, and he played in five Pro Bowl games, winning the Most Valuable Player award in the 1958 game. He finished out his career with Minnesota, the New York Giants, and Detroit, and his total yardage record added up to 11,375. McElhenny's average gain of 10.69 yards per carry in 1952 is still the second highest in league history.

There were a few people who criticized McElhenny as being "just a runner" in a pass-dominated pro game. Statistics belie this charge, for McElhenny caught 264 passes in his career, and when he retired after the 1964 season he was one of only three players to have gained more than 11,000 yards carrying the football—rushing, receiving, kickoff returns and punt returns. Of his 60 touchdowns, only 38 were scored on rushing plays, strong evidence of his versatility.

When asked about his fast running, about his fantastic sixth sense that seemed to warn him of imminent danger from a tackler, McElhenny would quip and say he did it because he was scared. He'd tell about the time, as a 6-year-old, he was in a pickup game on a Los Angeles lot when the owner arrived with a shotgun. A few pellets lodged in his backside.

"When I carry the ball, I think of that man and his shotgun," said McElhenny.

When asked what made him so good at ducking tacklers, he had this to say: "It's like walking down a dark alley. And you see at the end of the alley a glimmer of light from the cross street—that's the goal line—and you're desperately hurrying to get there.

"But on the way, even though the alley is so dark you can't see a thing, you sense a telegraph pole to your right and you sheer away from it. A few steps farther, you know there's a doorway with a man in it, even though you can't see him. You just feel it. So you turn away from that, too.

"Haven't you had that experience? I have. And, Lord, I'm glad to reach that cross street with the bright light—that goal line."

In 13 great pro seasons, his majesty, The King, reached that bright light many, many times.

Year	Team	G.	RUSHES Att.	Yds.	Avg.	TDs	RECEPTIONS No.	Yds.	Avg.	TDs
1952	San Fran.	12	98	684	7.0	6	26	367	14.1	3
1953	San Fran.	12	112	503	4.5	3	30	474	15.8	2
1954	San Fran.	6	64	515	8.0	6	8	162	20.3	0
1955	San Fran.	12	90	327	3.6	4	11	203	18.5	2
1956	San Fran.	12	185	916	5.0	8	16	193	12.1	0
1957	San Fran.	12	102	478	4.7	1	37	458	12.4	2
1958	San Fran.	12	113	451	4.0	6	31	366	11.8	2
1959	San Fran.	10	18	67	3.7	1	22	329	15.0	3
1960	San Fran.	9	95	347	3.7	0	14	114	8.1	1
1961	Minn.	13	120	570	4.8	3	37	283	7.6	3
1962	Minn.	11	50	200	4.0	0	16	191	11.9	0
1963	N.Y. Giants	14	55	175	3.2	0	11	91	8.3	2
1964	Detroit	8	22	48	2.2	0	5	16	3.2	0
Totals		143	1,124	5,281	4.7	38	264	3,247	12.3	20

Year	PUNT RETURNS No.	Yds.	Avg	TDs	KICKOFF RETURNS No.	Yds.	Avg.	TDs	SCORING TDs	Pts.
1952	20	284	14.2	1	18	396	22.0	0	10	60
1953	15	104	6.9	0	15	368	24.5	0	5	30
1954	8	78	9.8	0	8	210	26.3	0	6	36
1955	7	10	1.4	0	9	189	21.0	0	6	36
1956	15	38	2.5	0	13	300	23.1	0	8	48
1957	10	41	4.1	0	0	0	0.0	0	3	18
1958	24	93	3.9	0	2	31	15.5	0	8	48
1959	0	0	0.0	0	0	0	0.0	0	4	24
1960	0	0	0.0	0	0	0	0.0	0	1	6
1961	8	155	19.4	1	2	59	29.5	0	7	42
1962	5	43	8.6	0	7	160	22.9	0	0	0
1963	13	74	5.7	0	6	136	22.7	0	2	12
1964	1	0	0.0	0	3	72	24.0	0	0	0
Totals	126	920	7.3	2	83	1,921	23.1	0	60	360

UPI

Fights to break loose from ankle tackle against Cleveland Browns in 1966 NFL championship game.

Paul Hornung

Paul Hornung
by Joseph Durso

"You have to know what Hornung means to this team," Vince Lombardi was saying in *Run To Daylight*, his book of football memoirs. "I have heard and read that he is not a great runner or a great passer or a great field-goal kicker, although no one can fault him as a great blocker. But he led the league in scoring for three seasons; in 1960, he broke Don Hutson's all-time record with 176 points, and he was twice voted the league's outstanding player.

"In the middle of the field, he may be only slightly better than an average ballplayer. But inside that 20-yard line, he is one of the greatest I have ever seen. He smells that goal line."

Paul Vernon Hornung: an only child, born December 23, 1935, in Louisville, Kentucky, the son of a retired insurance agent. He was, his godmother remembered,

UPI
Plows over goal line, despite St. Louis Cardinal bear-hugging him around chest.

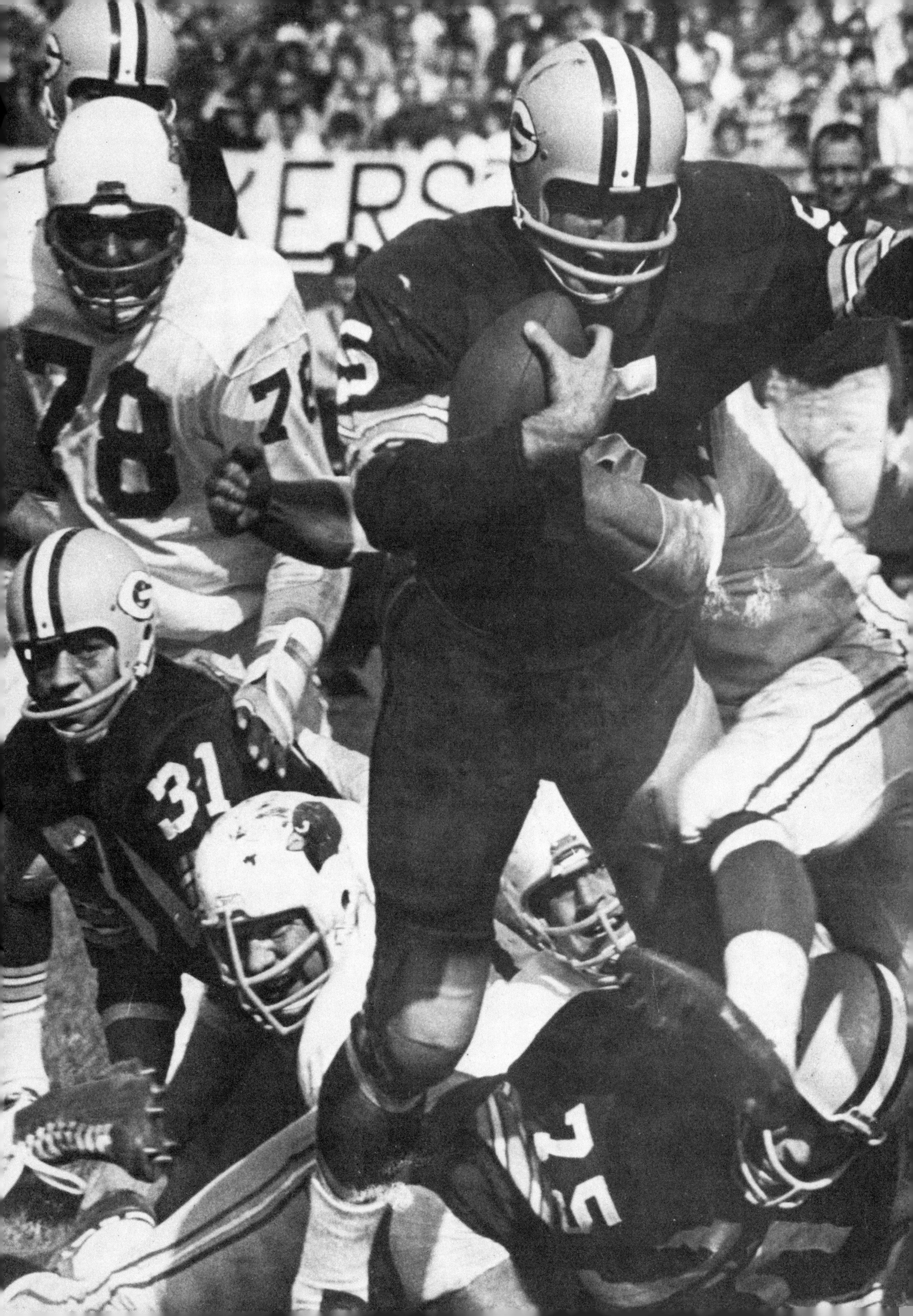
78
31

Hornung swings away from Chicago Bear defender during rugged 1960 game.

"a nice, large, lusty baby who liked to play with a ball in his crib." And 20 years later, the nice, large, lusty baby embarked on a career of playing with a ball in crowded stadiums for big money—under the disciplinarian of all time, Vince Lombardi.

"He didn't look the way I pictured him," Hornung recalled in *his* book later. "He didn't look coach-like. He wore glasses and he had this gentle kind of smile and he looked almost like a college professor: except that he was stocky and built tough and you could almost smell the toughness under that mild exterior."

So, in a marriage of true minds and absolutely conflicting spirits, Lombardi and Hornung formed one of the abiding alliances in football history—the demanding, stern, rigid coach of the Green Bay Packers and the cheerful, sunny-faced blond bon vivant from Notre Dame.

"Look at him," Lombardi suggested five years after their first meeting. "He may not be the greatest football player in the world, but the competitor never lived who came up bigger in the clutch."

"If Lombardi told me to move out wide on the next play, jump over the wall, land in the stands and buy a program," Hornung replied, "I think I would have done it."

The care and feeding of Paul Hornung, as well as the taming of him, did not become Lombardi's task until long after the chubby baby had graduated from crib to football field as one of the versatile athletes of postwar America. He went through St. Patrick's Elementary School in Louisville, then Flaget High School, where he played basketball, baseball and football. He considered going on to the University of Kentucky, but changed his mind after Flaget won the state football championship in 1952.

"It felt good playing with a winner," he reflected, "and I didn't want to change it. I figured the best way to get with a winner in college was by going to Notre Dame."

He figured right, though for a while during his freshman season he began to doubt that he'd even make the team. But Frank Leahy, the head coach, kept prompting him, let him practice with the varsity, and positioned him as the third-string quarterback the next year behind Ralph Guglielmi and Tom Carey. By his junior season, 1955, he was leading the team in passing, rushing, scoring and both kickoff and punt returns. He made all-American that year, while the Irish were winning eight of 10 games, and he made it the following year, when they were losing eight of 10 games.

He even wound up with the Heisman Trophy, as well as with a solid reputation as one of the academic world's true extroverts: 6-foot-3 and 210 pounds, compared with every culture idol from Adonis to Zeus, nicknamed the Golden Boy, and besieged with Hollywood contracts. Red Grange called him "the best running back I saw all year," and when he graduated just below the *cum laude* level, he declined the offers of Canadian teams and signed a three-year, $16,000-a-season contract with the Packers—Vince Lombardi's future team.

The only rub was that, in 1957, Lombardi was still an assistant coach with the New York Giants. So the grand alliance waited two years while Hornung squirmed under a succession of Green Bay chiefs. There was Lisle Blackbourn, who watched the bonus rookie in pre-season practice and decided that he couldn't pass well enough to become a quarterback, run hard enough to become a fullback, or run fast enough to become a halfback. There was Ray McLean, who struggled with so many problems besides Hornung that the Packers won only one game, tied one, and lost 10.

But the losing ended in 1959, when Lombardi appeared on the Green Bay scene. "He spoke with power," Hornung remembered. He also spoke with purpose, installing the happy bachelor as a running and passing halfback who promptly led the National Football League in scoring with 94 points while the Pack straightened out and won seven of 12 games.

In 1960, he scored a record total of 176 points and the Packers won eight of 12, plus their first Western Conference title in 16 years. It was Cinderella stuff for a team that had suffered through hard times, and Hornung's contribution was across the board: 15 touchdowns, 41 extra points, 15 field goals.

In the playoff game for the league title, though, the Philadelphia Eagles prevented any further heroics with a 17–13 decision. For most of the second half, the Packers played without their jack-of-all-trades because he was sidelined with a recurrence of an old injury, a pinched nerve in his neck that caused lack of control and feeling in his right arm.

Not only that, but he was sidelined for part of the 1961 season as well by the Army, which converted him to jeep driver and assigned him to Fort Riley, Kansas. Still, he managed to escape often enough to

UPI
Joe Schmidt, Lions' linebacker, on collision course with Hornung (above); Packers' star (below) races into the line to avoid Giants' Andy Robustelli (81).

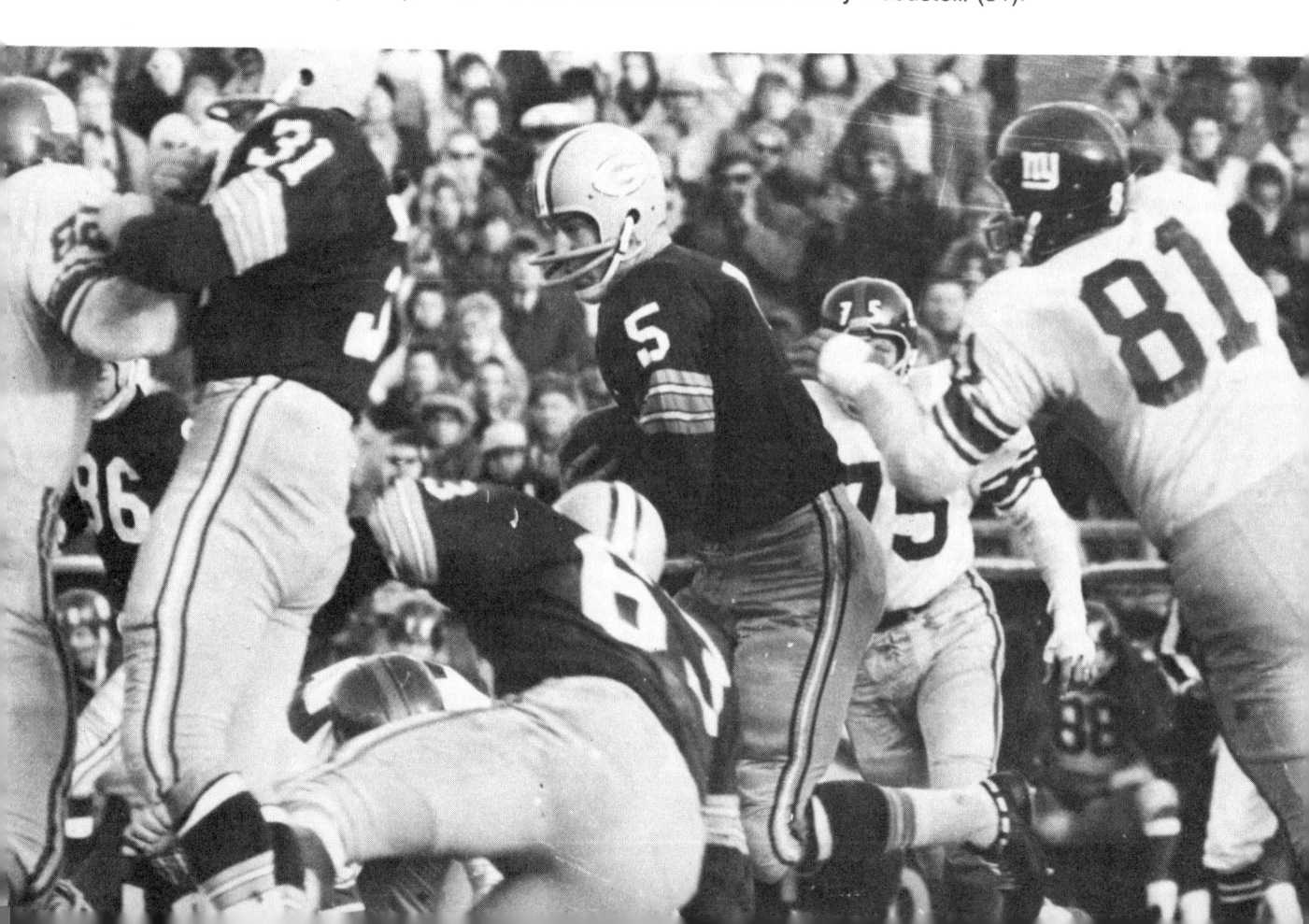

play in all but two games, thanks to a liberal weekend-pass policy and a private plane flown by a Green Bay fan. The Packers won 11 of 14 games, won the West again, and this time won the championship game over the Giants, 37–0, leaving few questions unanswered. Hornung's contribution this time was 146 points in the regular season, ranking him first in the NFL for the third straight year, plus 19 points in the title game.

There were times when it took a bit of lobbying to pry Paul loose from the jeep, lobbying that went up to the White House level. And among the duly impressed observers was Max McGee, the end who was Hornung's roommate for 10 years and who noted with wonder: "It took the President of the United States and the United States Army and Air Force to get Hornung to practice on time."

The following summer, his National Guard unit was deactivated and Hornung the jeep driver went back to full-time duty as Hornung the halfback. He celebrated by scoring 28 points in the opener against the Minnesota Vikings. Four weeks later he twisted his right knee and sat out the next six games. But Lombardi by now was surrounded with talent, losing only one of 14 games and beating the Giants again for the title, 16–7.

By now, the Golden Boy was earning close to $25,000 a year, he was driving a Cadillac, he shared a home in Green Bay with two teammates, and lived in the off-season with his mother in Louisville. He also was one of the stars on a team of stars, coached by a legend and entrenched as the football power of the Sixties. He had it made. But the wonderful world of the Packers was rattled in 1963 when Commissioner Pete Rozelle suspended Hornung and Alex Karras of the Detroit Lions for betting on pro games over the years at $100 or $200 (and occasionally $500) a crack.

"It was like a kick thing," Hornung said later. "This friend of mine was betting games and he'd call me, and I never told him to bet against us. Then one time I said, 'Bet me a hundred.' It seems like such a petty thing when you're doing it. Then, before the 1962 season started, the commissioner came to training camp and made it more emphatic about betting. I said to myself, 'This is silly, when you figure what you're risking on a wager every couple of weeks.'

"When the commissioner called me in, I wasn't scared. Even as a kid, if I was going to get whipped, I'd think, 'Well, tomorrow it won't hurt.' I went in there and told the truth. There was no use lying. Then the waiting started. It was the toughest three months I've ever known. Every time the phone would ring, I'd think: 'Is this it? Is it out now?' Every time I'd pick up a paper, I'd have the same feeling."

A year later, the suspension was lifted and Hornung got on the telephone, called Lombardi and said: "Suppose I move up to Green Bay and start working out right after the Kentucky Derby, the first week in May?" Lombardi replied: "Suppose you get here April 15?" And Hornung replied: "I'll compromise and be there on April 15."

During the next three months, he worked out by himself four times a week, doing a dozen laps around the practice field, striding 50 yards half a dozen times, running up all 60 steps in the stadium four times. He threw passes to Boyd Dowler; he caught passes thrown to him by Bart Starr. He was 28 years old, and what next?

"Normally, a year's layoff would affect an athlete," said Fuzzy Thurston, the guard. "But knowing Paul, I'll predict he'll come back as strong as ever."

"Pride is the greatest asset an athlete can have," said Starr, the quarterback. "I hardly believe Hornung would let a year's layoff affect him physically as well as mentally."

UPI

Hornung tries to get away from Richie Petitbon, Chicago Bears' defensive back (17).

"If Hornung wants to pay the price, he'll be as good as ever," said George Allen, then the defensive coach of the Chicago Bears. "When Mr. Lombardi gets through with Paul, he'll be ready."

He was ready, but the violent world of pro football had moved ahead of him during that year of running laps, and Hornung spent his remaining days in the NFL laboring to catch the clock. By the following season, it looked as if he might not catch anybody, especially the Paul Hornung who had ruled the roost. Going into the home stretch of the 1965 season, he had gained only 231 yards, had scored only 18 points, and had won himself a seat on the Green Bay bench. There was even talk that the Packers would make him available in the player pool to stock the new franchise in Atlanta.

Then, on December 12, in the fog in Baltimore, he was unleashed by Lombardi in a critical game against the Colts. It was played at the end of a week of solitude imposed by Lombardi: a lonely hotel 20 miles outside Baltimore, where the Packers lived like hermits, drank soft drinks only, and responded personally when the coach made the bed check.

Then, with the season at stake on Sunday, they broke loose as Hornung made one of the dramatic comebacks on record. He rushed for only 61 yards, but the yards came in telling spurts: two yards through left guard for a touchdown, ten yards around left end for a touchdown, three more through left guard for a touchdown. He also caught two touchdown passes for 115 yards, the final one breaking a Colt rally with 5½ minutes to play. On third-and-nine from the Green Bay 35, Hornung slanted across the middle, clutched Starr's short pass and burst the rest of the way on a 65-yard play.

"Clean living," he reflected later with a wink. "I owe it all to clean living."

The clean living paid off again in the championship game against the Cleveland Browns, and that was the last hurrah. A year later, he was drafted by the New Orleans Saints, another expansion club, where he was reunited with his old fullback, Jim Taylor. But the pinched nerve in Hornung's size-18 neck led to a medical decision not to tempt fate, and the curtain rang down after 760 points and a decade of Packer football.

Later, leading the life of a football broadcaster and restaurant owner, Hornung was asked how he felt about the "dehumanizing" aspect of football as described by several players who had quit with critical second-thoughts about it all.

"You can be 'dehumanized' by any business if you let it," he said. "The coach used to holler at me more than, say, a Jimmy Taylor or a Ron Kramer. He knew I wouldn't let it bother me. I don't regret anything I did. If I did it over again, I would go to Notre Dame, the Hula Bowl, the Super Bowl, and the Green Bay Packers."

Year	Team	G.	RUSHES Att.	Yds.	Avg.	TDs	RECEPTIONS No.	Yds.	Avg.	TDs
1957	Green Bay	12	60	319	5.3	3	6	34	5.7	0
1958	Green Bay	12	69	310	4.5	2	15	137	9.1	0
1959	Green Bay	12	152	681	4.5	7	15	113	7.5	0
1960	Green Bay	12	160	671	4.2	13	28	257	9.2	2
1961	Green Bay	12	127	597	4.7	8	15	145	9.7	2
1962	Green Bay	9	57	219	3.8	5	9	168	18.7	2
1964	Green Bay	14	103	415	4.0	5	9	98	10.9	0
1965	Green Bay	12	89	299	3.4	5	19	336	17.7	3
1966	Green Bay	9	76	200	2.6	2	14	192	13.7	3
Totals		104	893	3,711	4.2	50	130	1,480	11.4	12

Year	PASSES Att.	Comp.	Pct.	Yds.	TDs	Int.	SCORING TDs	XP	FG	Pts.
1957	6	1	16.7	−1	0	0	3	0	0	18
1958	1	0	0.0	0	0	0	2	22	11	67
1959	8	5	62.5	95	2	0	7	31	7	94
1960	16	6	37.5	118	2	0	15	41	15	176
1961	5	3	60.0	42	1	0	10	41	15	146
1962	6	4	66.7	80	0	2	7	14	6	74
1964	10	3	30.0	25	0	1	5	41	12	107
1965	2	1	50.0	19	0	1	8	0	0	48
1966	1	1	100.0	5	0	0	5	0	0	30
Totals	55	24	43.6	383	5	4	62	190	66	760

UPI

Battles for extra yard in 1966 title game against a host of Cowboys, including Dave Edwards (52), Chuck Howley (54), Jim Colvin (77), and George Andrie (66).

Jim Taylor

Jim Taylor
by Thomas Rogers

"You've got to sting 'em," was James Charles Taylor's credo during the ten years he was terrorizing National Football League defensive units.

And sting 'em he did. The 6-foot, 215-pound fullback gained 8,597 yards and scored 93 touchdowns, mostly on bull-like blasts through and over tacklers usually much bigger and heavier than himself.

A physical-fitness fanatic who toughened his body through weight lifting, isometric exercises, and Spartan training habits, Taylor was the epitome of the bread-and-butter runner, the kind who could be counted on to get two or three yards when they were most needed.

Not a remarkably fast back, he relied on short, piston-like leg action, combined with a head-down charge and sheer determination to advance the ball.

UPI

Lions' Joe Schmidt (56) and Sam Williams (88) prepare to converge on Packers' hard-running fullback.

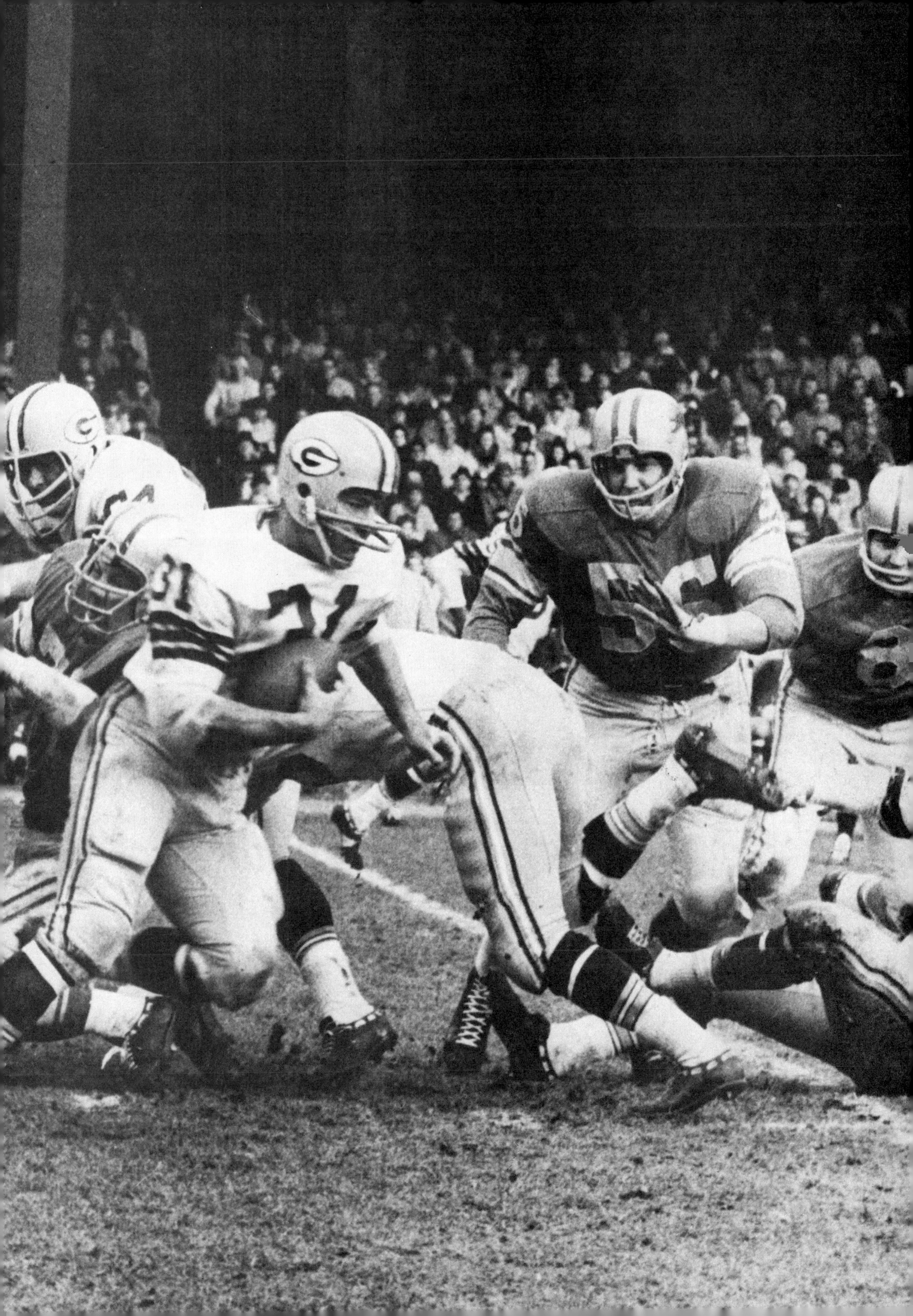

"He'll kill you for a yard," said one opposing lineman.

Hank Gremminger, a defensive back and teammate of Taylor's with the Green Bay Packers, studied his running style for several seasons and came to the following conclusions:

"There is an area where no one in the league can hit Taylor—or get hit by Taylor —and stop him. That's between his knees and hips. Anyone who tries to stop him there gets murdered. The only sure way a defensive halfback can bring Taylor down is hit him around the ankles. The big linemen can get him by coming down on him from above."

Taylor played nine seasons with the Packers, and during that time they compiled a dazzling record: five division titles, four NFL championships, and the first Super Bowl victory.

The former Louisiana State University star received his share of credit for most of those achievements, but, admittedly, he was fortunate to play under Vince Lombardi and to be surrounded by a collection of other superb athletes.

Taylor's first pro season in 1958 was an inauspicious one, both for him and the Packers who suffered under Coach Ray ("Scooter") McLean through a 12-game schedule. They managed to win only once.

Taylor was the team's second draft choice, but he did not impress McLean, who used him infrequently (mostly on the specialty teams) and subjected him to frequent tongue-lashings.

"It got so that I was scared to move," Taylor remembered.

Taylor finally fit into the Green Bay offense well enough to start the final two games of the season in San Francisco and Los Angeles. He averaged more than 100 yards in each game. Lucky he did, for the Packers brought Lombardi on the scene for the next season, and the new head coach studied the films of the West Coast games.

"It was tough evaluating him because he had played so little," Lombardi recalled. "He was a bit lax out there and his blocking was poor, but you could see that he hit well and had the knack for finding the hole. Also, he had fine balance. He's not the fastest runner around, nor the biggest, but he has the best balance."

Lombardi paired Taylor and Paul Hornung as running backs, behind the quarterbacking of Bart Starr, and this backfield combination became one of the most formidable offensive machines in the history of the league.

Taylor banged up the middle and Hornung swept the ends. When the defense moved up to stop the running attack, Starr took to the air, his pinpoint passing taking advantage of the openings.

For his feats in the 1962 season—he rolled up 1,474 yards—Taylor was the most valuable player in the NFL. But perhaps his greatest achievement, one unequaled in league history, was exceeding the important 1,000-yard rushing total for five consecutive years, 1960 through 1964.

For a smallish fullback who so relished punishing physical contact, it was remarkable that he could survive five NFL years in which he threw himself into the line more than 230 times a season.

"I love to hit a man," he said. "It's not that I want to hurt anyone, but if I have the ball and I'm running and the linebacker comes at me and I try to finesse him out of the way, and he won't finesse, then I must run into him, over him or through him.

"You've got to sting 'em. If you give a guy a little blast, maybe the next time he won't be so eager. Football is a game of contact. You've got to make them respect you. You've got to punish them before they punish you. You try to give more than you take. It's either them or you."

"Taylor is a crazy runner," said Dick

UPI
Jim Taylor drives past Cowboys' Jim Colvin (77) in memorable 1966 title game won by Green Bay, 34-27.

Jim Taylor plunges into line as Norm Masters (78) puts block on Sam Williams of Detroit Lions (88).

UPI

Jim Taylor looks back after he scores on 35-yard run in 1964 Pro Bowl game.

Modzelewski, a bulky tackle for the New York Giants. "You'll knock him down and he'll get up and say, 'Is that the hardest you can hit me?' "

"Jim will let you grab a leg," said Bill Austin when he was an assistant coach at Green Bay, "then ram it through your chest."

Taylor once surprised five Ram players after they had landed on him and mauled him enough to finish most runners for the afternoon.

Taylor leaped to his feet, clapped his hands and said to the Ram tacklers, "Way to hustle, guys!"

Much of Taylor's physical prowess stemmed from a hard-working childhood in Baton Rouge, Louisiana, where life began for him on September 20, 1935.

His father died when Jim was in grade school and his mother had to work in a laundry to support Jim and two brothers. He took on two paper routes. The first one required Jim to get up before dawn. The other one he worked after school.

"I must have pedaled my bike a million miles," said Taylor, looking back, "and it must have done my leg muscles some good."

While in high school, he developed his upper body as a "roughneck" on an offshore oil rig, handling heavy pipes.

"It was the toughest thing I ever did," he decided. "We'd go out there by boat for 10 or 12 hours and sometimes come back

76

with our lunch unopened because we hadn't had time to eat. The pay was good—$250 to $300 a week—but it was a tough way to get it."

Taylor eventually found it easier (and more fun) to bowl over 270-pound linemen and smash defensive backs into the turf.

By the time he entered Louisiana State, Taylor was a physical marvel, excelling in basketball and football. But, after an impressive freshman year in football, he flunked out.

"I didn't study at all in high school," he said. "The teachers just passed me through. I didn't know how to study."

He learned how to study at Hinds Junior College in Raymond, Mississippi, where he met Dixie Jo Pyron, who soon became his wife. After two years, he reapplied at LSU and played two seasons under Paul Dietzel. Although he was overshadowed in college by Billy Cannon, the Packers were impressed enough to make him their second draft choice.

When Vince Lombardi arrived, Taylor started to get attention, although he missed much of Lombardi's first season because of a kitchen accident in which he was horribly burned by hot grease. But not before he had picked up 452 yards in 120 carries.

Then, in 1960, he started the string of 1,000-plus yards. The Packer machine became overpowering.

One of the few frustrations of Taylor's career (but a big one) were the constant comparisons with Jim Brown, the Cleveland star generally regarded as the best running back in the sport.

As a result, Taylor usually put out a little extra against Cleveland and had some exceptional games against the Browns. Perhaps his finest was on October 15, 1961, in Cleveland.

A crowd of 75,042 saw Taylor score four touchdowns and gain 158 yards, 33 more than the whole Cleveland offense. The Packers won, 49–17, and held Brown to 72 yards in 16 carries.

"Who's Jim Brown?" cracked Hornung in the locker room.

"I never saw a fullback have a day like Taylor had today," Brown was forced to admit.

Besides doing well against Brown in head-to-head meetings, Taylor also felt he was a more complete player, especially in regard to blocking.

Lombardi had worked hard on Taylor and had made him one of the best blockers in the league. The Packers' coach concentrated on one block in particular, a crab block, in which Taylor would throw his whole body low at the defender, with both hands and both legs on the ground.

"Jim Brown doesn't know anything about a crab block," said Taylor. "It's all news to him. Blocking is a matter of making up your mind to get the job done. You can't figure on saving yourself for the run. When the play calls for a block, you gotta block."

In addition to his acknowledged superiority to Brown in blocking, Taylor was also considered a tougher runner to bring down than Brown by some experts on the subject.

"The impact of meeting Taylor after five yards is greater than meeting Brown at the same point," said Sam Huff, one of the great middle linebackers of Taylor's era. "Brown is strong, but he doesn't shock you like Taylor does."

Huff and Taylor had a memorable confrontation in the 1962 championship game at Yankee Stadium where the Packers hacked out a 16–7 victory. Taylor, although suffering from sore ribs, carried the ball 31 times, and scored the game's only touchdown.

Huff and the Giants keyed on Taylor, who was about 10 pounds under his normal weight, and dealt him a full load of punish-

UPI
Packers' fullback rams through hole over right guard for touchdown against Lions.

ment. He left the field late in the game, spitting blood from a gashed tongue, and was taken immediately to a hospital.

The violent crunches between Taylor and Huff brought forth a cascade of letters from television viewers, most of whom accused Huff of dirty tactics. The Packer runner and the Giant linebacker also engaged in a publicized feud, Taylor doing his talking from his bed in Baton Rouge where he was recovering from an attack of hepatitis.

The hepatitis and the one-year suspension of Hornung made the 1963 season a challenging one for Taylor. Weakened by the disease and forced to carry the Packers' running game almost single-handed, he still ground out 1,018 yards.

In 1964, with Hornung back, Taylor set the record of five straight seasons of more than 1,000 yards as he rushed for 1,169 yards.

A torn Achilles tendon suffered in the last preseason game before the 1965 season prevented Taylor from extending his remarkable string. Unable to run with his customary drive, he finished the regular season with 734 yards. Rumors began floating around that he was no longer the feared runner he had been.

In the championship game against the Browns on January 2, 1966, Taylor proved that he could still be his old destructive self in a big game. He charged across a snowy field in Green Bay for 96 yards in 27 carries.

The Packers held Brown to 50 yards on 12 attempts and the Packers won another crown, 23–12.

But Lombardi began preparing for the day when Taylor and Hornung would not be available to lead his ground attack and signed Donnie Anderson and Jim Grabowski for huge bonuses. There was resentment from Taylor.

"It's kind of ridiculous to pay sometimes twice as much for doing half the job," he said. "It has to cause hard feelings."

He played out his option during the 1966 season and then signed a multi-year contract with the New Orleans Saints.

Playing with an expansion team and behind a weak offensive line, Taylor gained only 390 yards for the Saints in 1967 and decided to end his career.

He finished with 8,597 yards (second only to Brown in career rushing) in 1,941 carries for an average of 4.4 yards a carry. Darned good for a back that Lombardi once thought was a bit lax!

Year	Team	G.	RUSHES Att.	Yds.	Avg.	TDs	RECEPTIONS No.	Yds.	Avg.	SCORING TDs	TDs	Pts.
1958	Green Bay	12	52	247	4.8	1	4	72	18.0	1	2	12
1959	Green Bay	12	120	452	3.8	6	9	71	7.9	2	8	48
1960	Green Bay	12	230	1,101	4.8	11	15	121	8.1	0	11	66
1961	Green Bay	14	243	1,307	5.4	15	25	175	7.0	1	16	96
1962	Green Bay	14	272	1,474	5.4	19	22	106	4.8	0	19	114
1963	Green Bay	14	248	1,018	4.1	9	13	68	5.2	1	10	60
1964	Green Bay	13	235	1,169	5.0	12	38	354	9.3	3	15	90
1965	Green Bay	13	207	734	3.5	4	20	207	10.4	0	4	24
1966	Green Bay	14	204	705	3.5	4	41	331	8.1	2	6	36
1967	New Orleans	14	130	390	3.0	2	38	251	6.6	0	2	12
Totals		132	1,941	8,597	4.4	83	225	1,756	7.8	10	93	558

UPI

Hunts for running room as Marion Rushing (52) leads pack of St. Louis Cardinals chasing him.

Jim Brown

Jim Brown

by George DeGregorio

"I loved those long sweeps. Once I was through the hole and into the other team's secondary, that's when I was on my own. Then I had a one-on-one situation going—me against them; that's when I'd go into my bag of stuff. They're in trouble now—I'm in their territory; 55 things happening at once; I'm moving, evaluating their possible moves, trying to outthink and outmaneuver them, using my speed, quickness and balance. I'm ready to use a straight-arm, or just the forearm, then the shoulder."

In those words Jim Brown described in a *Playboy* magazine interview how he became the most indestructible running back in the history of pro football during nine spectacular seasons with the Cleveland Browns.

His long sweep was a thing of such

UPI

Trapped at scrimmage line as Steelers' Joe Krupa grabs him around waist.

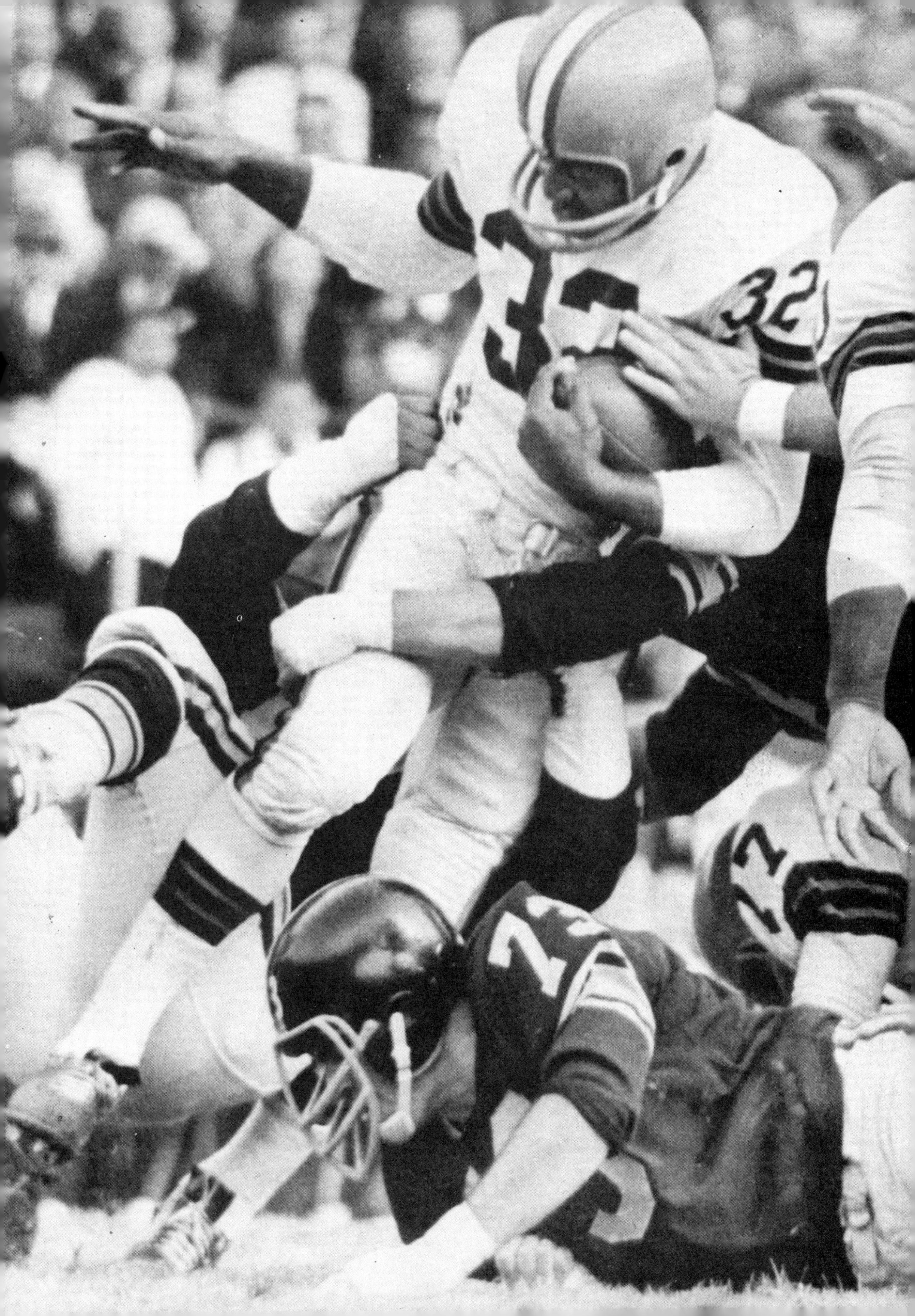

beauty and devastation as he piled up a record career total of 12,312 yards that it became the artistic source material for writers and cameramen eager to chronicle his feats or capture visually the superb rhythm of his limber muscles on Sunday afternoons.

In many ways Brown's description of himself in action was also the model for his approach to life—as superstar, actor, businessman, and black civil rights activist. Few black football players before him had won such unanimous accolades for ability; few had been so outspoken and militant in their stand to gain equal treatment for black players; none had made the successful transition from athlete to bona fide movie star.

"In the leg maneuvers, I'd limber leg, offering one leg, then jerking it away when somebody grabbed," Brown continued. "Or high-stepping would keep a pair of tacklers from getting both legs at once. In that secondary, it was just a step-by-step thing, using brainwork and instinct; but sometimes it got down to just out-and-out strength and brute force."

Brown's quickness as a runner was unusual for a man his size. He stood 6 feet 2 inches and weighed 228 pounds at his playing best. But on his own or behind a screen of blockers Brown offered the defense the ultimate challenge: First try to reach him and then try to bring him down.

"In one-on-one situations," he has said, "you break guys into categories. If he's a lineman and he's four yards away, you figure to put a good move on him and go around. A linebacker is quicker and therefore harder to fake. If he is three yards or less away, you drop your shoulder and struggle. If he's a small defensive back, you just run right over him."

Sam Huff, the great New York Giants'

UPI
Jim Brown slides off mass pile-up of Cardinals and scores in 1968 game.

linebacker, once was asked how he went about trying to stop Brown. "All you can do is grab hold, hang on, and wait for help," Huff said. Alex Karras, the fabled all-pro Detroit Lions tackle, summed up the frustration and desperation of most opponents with this advice: "Give each guy in the line an ax."

Some critics have said that Brown, who carried the ball 25 to 30 times a game, was called upon for more running duty than was expected of a fullback. For the first six years of his pro career he was playing under a doctrinaire system prescribed by Paul Brown, a strongly opinionated, unflappable coach who called virtually all the Cleveland plays from the sidelines. Coach Brown believed that if you had a big, strong man like Jim Brown who could crack the line for five or more yards every time he carried the ball, by all means he should be used as often as possible. In the Cleveland attack, 30 carries by Brown represented half of the team's total offensive plays for a single game.

In his nine years with the Browns, Jim carried the ball 2,359 times, more than anyone else in pro football history. His average per carry was an incredible 5.22 yards. He produced 106 touchdowns by rushing and 126 in all, including those scored on passes —both National Football League records. His single-season record of 1,863 yards and his career total seem likely to last longest. His single-game high of 237 yards was achieved twice (the first time in his rookie season), and it was the league standard until Willie Ellison, then playing with Los Angeles, broke it by gaining 247 yards in 1971. In all, Brown set 15 NFL records, and during his time he was the highest paid player at $75,000 a year.

Brown's speed, power and balance emanated from his superb physical endowments—broad shoulders tapering down to a 32-inch waistline, then bulging into two massive tremendously muscular thighs. To make himself lighter and faster, he wore no hip pads, and his thigh protectors were stripped to the basic plastic.

He was the Browns' No. 1 draft choice in 1957 out of Syracuse University, where he was a unanimous all-America selection. His adjustment to the pro game was instantaneous (he beat out Ed ("Big Mo") Modzelewski, a rugged fullback, for the job) and went on to be the NFL's unanimous choice as rookie of the year. He won the rushing title with 942 yards in 202 carries and scored 10 touchdowns. (Modzelewski was to say later: "I felt like I was playing behind Babe Ruth.")

It was the start of a record five straight rushing titles. Only once—in 1962—during his nine seasons did he fail to win the rushing crown and only twice did he miss the 1,000-yard mark. The year he lost the title he carried for 996 yards and scored 18 touchdowns, finishing second to Jim Taylor of the Green Bay Packers.

A proud player, fiercely determined to be the best at his profession, Brown was irked following the 1962 season by criticism that perhaps he was losing his place as football's premier runner.

"I'm no superman," Brown answered the critics. "I had a good season—not a great one, though. Do I have to lead the league every time for it to be a good year? Just because somebody else gained more yards doesn't mean I was poor. I don't like to boast, but I think I'm as good as anyone in this league as an all-round offensive player."

The Cleveland Browns, before Jim Brown came on the scene, had been the winningest team in pro football. Despite Paul Brown's moodiness and his dictatorial ways in telling his players how to behave on and off the field, the Browns had won seven league championships—four in the old All-America Conference and three in the NFL —in 10 years. But since 1955, although they had taken several division titles, the Browns had been shut out from the big prize.

Coach Brown clung stubbornly to his old prescriptions, refusing to change methods or to treat his men like pros. "We will be the most amateur team in professional sports," he once told his players. "I want you to think of the game first and the money second."

Jim Brown's performance in 1962 was under par by his own standards, but he defended it. He was dissatisfied with being the No. 2 rusher in the league, even for one season. Part of this dissatisfaction stemmed from his disenchantment with conditions under Coach Brown. The resentment also grew among a majority of the players.

"We were a mechanical club," Jim said. "I'm the kind of player who must perform freely, be relaxed. After so many years it's an established fact that a player should know a little about the game. When this isn't recognized, it's hopeless."

A group of Cleveland players went to see Art Modell, the team's new owner, and presented their case—in effect, indicting the coach for creating a breakdown in morale. Jim Brown put himself in the center of the storm, hinting that if there were no change he would retire from football. He said he was being asked to do "more than my share" and that he was faced with a business opportunity that "might be too important" to miss.

Modell, eager to win a championship himself, dismissed Brown as coach and moved him into the front office. The man to replace him was Blanton Collier, who had been an assistant under Brown and was aware of the players' dissatisfaction. Collier was considered a tolerant, warm, friendly, and democratic coach, capable of extracting extra effort from his players. He and Jim Brown always got along.

Through it all, Jim Brown refused

UPI
Jim Brown on his way to 13-yard run against Eagles in 1961 game in which he set rushing mark of 242 yards and made four touchdowns.

directly to criticize Paul Brown. "Anybody who says that I'm trying to show up Paul Brown is small-minded," he said. "I don't look back unless somebody forces me to. I've always given my best, even when I didn't believe in what I was being asked to do. But I always felt that there were ways to make what I have work better. Now I have the opportunity."

Collier increased Jim's value to the team. He put into effect the option-block system used at Green Bay. In this system the linemen got the choice of blocking either in or out, depending on how a man's opponent moved. Under the Paul Brown system, a

Jim Brown shifts stride to evade a tackler as Lions' Roger Brown (76), Wayne Walker (55), and Dennis Gaubatz (53) try to catch Cleveland's premier fullback.

lineman blocked only in one designated direction, regardless of what the defensive player did. For Jim Brown the new system was perfect. He called it "instinctive football"—he would be able to read the blocking and react accordingly.

In this new atmosphere, Jim Brown, who received most of the publicity as the ringleader in bringing down the palace guard, came smashing back in the 1963 season.

He set his single season rushing mark, caught 24 passes, and scored 15 touchdowns. Besides being named all-pro (every year he played), he was singled out as player of the year, received the Bert Bell Memorial Award, and was asked to be a social guest at the White House by President Lyndon B. Johnson.

The Browns, however, failed to win the league crown and Jim Brown once again was the target of the critics. He was taken to task for not doing his share of the blocking. His retort to the critics (Otto Graham, the quarterback of the Browns' glory days, was foremost among them) was simple: "I simply wasn't cast to do blocking in the Browns' system. Our offense was geared for me to run. I think I had six blocking assignments in our whole repertoire of plays. I always tried to satisfy the coach I worked for and running was what they always asked of me."

The next year Jim Brown paved the way for the Browns to go all the way and win the NFL title. He ran for 1,446 yards that season and in the title game slashed through for 114 yards in a 27–0 rout of the favored Baltimore Colts. In 1965, Brown's last season, the Browns won their second straight Eastern crown, and their third since Brown spurred them to division honors in his rookie campaign.

Brown's greatest game? It would be hard to choose. There were many, including a five-touchdown performance against the Colts in 1959 and a four-touchdown show against the Los Angeles Rams in his record-breaking 237-yard rushing game during his

UPI
Redskins' defensive back holds on to Jim Brown as Ralph Felton runs over.

rookie year. He was always great against the tough teams.

In New York, in 1963, against the defending Eastern champion Giants, Brown was unmatchable. The Browns were trailing, 17–14, when Brown, who had scored in the first half, took charge early in the third period. He caught a short screen pass and, faking out a platoon of defenders, went 72 yards for a score. Minutes later, taking a handoff, he went to his left, reversed field and churned 32 yards for another tally, beating the Giants single-handed.

He was like a home-run hitter who could break open any game in the late innings.

Throughout his career Brown played with the reputation of being so tough he couldn't be hurt. Although he once suffered a concussion, he was never hurt so badly as to stay out of action for long. In nine years he never missed a game and was never out for more than a period or two. He played most of 1962 with an injured wrist and during his career received many cuts, bruises and strains. Because it often took two, three, and sometimes four men to bring him down, Brown was always in collision with big, 260-pound linemen who were trying to put him out of action or in a hospital bed. After a game it would take him several days to recuperate, or "thaw out," from the battering he had taken. A round of golf (he shot in the 70's) would usually loosen him up. He said his hands suffered most from the heavy contact. "See those scars," he has said. "I still can't shake hands with much grip; can't even get an ordinary grip on a doorknob. I got hit on a nerve once."

Hall of Fame

Brown leaps up and goes over goal line, despite efforts of Bill Pellington, Colts' linebacker (36), as Cleveland wins 1964 championship, 27-0

Brown's use of his body to struggle away from would-be tacklers should have increased his chances of being injured, but in fact it became a weapon in his favor.

Matt Hazeltine, the San Francisco 49ers' linebacker, speaking of Brown's forearm smashes, put it this way: "Brown really shivers you. I wonder how many KO's he would have scored when there were no face masks?"

Brown's resentment over players who tried to retaliate with dirty tactics was at its greatest when they went for his face and eyes.

"One time, I remember, a Philadelphia Eagles' defenseman jammed his hand up under my face mask; I felt him clawing for my eyes and I got my teeth in that hand. Man, I tried to eat it up! I'll bet it hasn't run under any more masks since then.

Later, there was a protest about my biting him. I said, 'Look, I can't bite anybody through a mask, can I? Any hand under there was under there for some purpose, right?' "

Brown also carried with him throughout his career a reputation for being aloof, removed from his teammates and fans and, in fact, sometimes appearing reticent, moody and rude with reporters, especially at gametime.

"Maybe I was rude to people and had very little to say to anybody," Brown has said. "The reason is that I was focused mentally on that coming game. I was concentrating, visualizing things that I knew could happen, and what I would do if it went this way or that way. Every play I ever ran I had already run a thousand times in my mind."

89

James Nathaniel Brown was born off the coast of Georgia, on St. Simons Island, on February 17, 1936. Although he was to become the Emperor Jones of black football superstars, there was no halo over his head and no silver spoon in his mouth at birth to herald the fame and wealth his athletic exploits would bring him. The Brown household was hard-pressed for money and down on its luck. His father was an amateur boxer and golf caddie who liked to gamble, a playboy without funds who was more fond of carousing than raising a family. When Jim was born, his parents separated, and when he was two years old his mother left him with a great-grandmother in order to move north to find domestic work. She settled in Manhasset, Long Island. When Jim was seven, he was sent north to rejoin her, taking with him memories shaped on St. Simons of rock fights with white boys, segregated schooling and "whites-only" beaches.

At Manhasset High School, Jim Brown became a legend. He won 13 varsity letters in five sports. He was an All-State player in football, basketball and track. In football he was a first-stringer at the age of 14 and he established a fantastic record of 14.9 yards a carry. He was equally tough on defense—in his final game he made seven tackles in 11 plays against Garden City (L.I.) High to assure Manhasset of its first unbeaten season in 29 years.

In basketball he averaged 38 points a game, once scoring 55 to break the record held by Carl Braun, who became a star player for the New York Knicks and Boston Celtics. He played lacrosse and was a pitcher and first baseman on the baseball team, attracting offers from the New York Yankees and Boston Braves.

On top of his sports accomplishments, Brown distinguished himself among his classmates. He was a B-minus student, and although his mother worked as a domestic in the homes of some of the students, they elected him class president and chief justice of the student court.

By this time word of this "super" athlete spread throughout the nation. Forty-four colleges offered him full four-year athletic scholarships.

It would seem that a player who had 44 colleges clamoring for his talents would have no problems. But Brown had his hang-ups. Although he excelled on the field, he was a strong individualist. His broken-home background had made him introspective and sensitive, often a loner, and he was generally suspicious of white people.

In high school Jim was befriended by a lawyer named Ken Mulloy, an alumnus of Syracuse University, who was eager to make a catch for the upstate New York school. Mulloy started a campaign to get Brown a scholarship at Syracuse, but the university turned him down, offering him instead a conditional deal. If Brown proved his value during the freshman football season, he would be granted a scholarship during his sophomore year. Mulloy was determined that Brown should go to Syracuse. Along with several Manhasset civic leaders who thought highly of Jim, Mulloy contributed to a fund to underwrite Brown's tuition and expenses for his first year of college.

Brown was unaware of the arrangement, but in later years when he was to know the details his criticism of Syracuse officials was sharp—yet his loyalty and devotion to Mulloy remained unswerving.

At Syracuse, despite Mulloy's hard work to get Jim Brown there, the coaches seemed to have a blind spot. They were at first unable or unwilling to recognize the talent Mulloy had found for them. Throughout Brown's first year, the coaches didn't want him as a starting player on the freshman team, and with almost half the season gone in his sophomore year he was still among

UPI
Jim Brown hurdles a teammate and Eagles move in.

the fourth- and fifth-stringers on the varsity squad. The reason?

"I was black, that's why," Brown has said. "You see, before I went to Syracuse, a Negro named Avatus Stone had been a great ballplayer there—a quarterback, a great punter. They wanted him to play end, but he refused and finally left and went to Canada. But the real rub was that Stone had been very popular among white coeds —which made him very unpopular with white males. So when I arrived, the only black man on the team, the coaches had nothing to say to me except 'Don't be like Avatus Stone!' My whole freshman year, I heard so many sermons about what I should be like, I got so many hang-ups, that my attitude became as bad as theirs."

Because he did not have an athletic scholarship, Brown did not live in the players' dormitory or eat his meals with them. He was becoming so withdrawn and playing so little that he thought more and more of switching to another school. But Mulloy convinced him to try harder and to stay at Syracuse.

"I hustled like mad when sophomore training season opened," Brown has said. "I got in a few games, but nothing spectacular happened until, finally, in the fourth game against Illinois, we had a lot of injuries on the team and I started. We got badly beaten, but I carried 13 times, averaging five yards, and the fans caught that. When I was on the bench, they started hollering, 'We want Brown! Brown!

UPI
Brown pivots away from Ralph Heck (43), Eagles' linebacker, and scores.

Brown!' Man, that made me feel ten feet tall."

Brown's big break that season came against Cornell. Although the Orange lost, 14–6, he made a long touchdown run and gained 150 yards. In the next game, against Colgate, he scored twice and became an overnight on-campus celebrity. And he was now on full scholarship.

"In my junior year I started thinking I had it made, and Pittsburgh bottled me up for 28 yards in 12 carries. The coaches demoted me to second team. That made me so mad I saw fire; and in the next practice scrimmage, I left first-string tacklers lying all over the field and ran four touchdowns in five plays. After that, they left me on the first string. That's how I got accepted. I mean accepted as Jim Brown, not Avatus Stone. Once the coaches made up their minds, they were men enough to realize they had been wrong and they became fair in dealing with me, and then I gave it all I had."

By the time Brown's senior year rolled around, Syracuse had risen to national prominence and was drumbeating for a Bowl bid. The selection committees, however, were wary because the Orange in previous Bowl appearances had been unimpressive. Against Colgate, in the season finale, Brown led the Orange to a 67–6 victory, scoring an unbelievable 43 points on six touchdowns and seven placement kicks and gaining 197 yards. The performance wrapped up an invitation to the Cotton Bowl.

At Dallas, Brown opened more eyes with a scintillating running exhibition, although Syracuse lost a thriller to Texas Christian, 28–27. But Brown had rushed for 132 yards and scored 21 points on national television. He became everybody's all-American.

In virtually all the media, sports experts were calling Jim Brown the greatest all-around athlete since Jim Thorpe. He had cut a wide path of excellence in lacrosse and track, attaining all-America honors in lacrosse, a game he was so fond of that he said he would like to play five days a week. He once fired a ball so hard it tore through the opposing goaltender's net.

As a sophomore, he placed fifth in the national decathlon championships. The performance would have made him a certain choice for the United States Olympic team in 1956, but he passed up the chance, explaining later: "It wouldn't have been fair. I was in Syracuse on a football scholarship, and the Olympics would have cut into the time I was committed to give to football."

Brown played in 43 varsity basketball games for the Orange and scored 563 points. Although he did not compete in his senior year, he was so highly thought of in that sport that the Syracuse Nationals of the National Basketball Association drafted him. In all, he earned 10 letters—three each in football and lacrosse, and two each in basketball and track.

Roy Simmons, the Syracuse boxing and lacrosse coach, said he could have developed Brown into the intercollegiate champion if he had joined the boxing team. And Norman Rothschild, a Syracuse boxing promoter, was so convinced of Jim's potential as the heavyweight champion that he offered him a three-year $150,000 contract when he graduated if he would go into pro boxing.

Said Simmons, in summing up Brown's athletic prowess: "Name the game and he'll play it like a pro in 48 hours. He could be all-American in anything from tiddlywinks to football."

Brown's off-season interests and his drive to excel eventually put him into show business. He started as host for a small radio show in Cleveland, then got his first movie role in "Rio Concho," a Western released in 1964 by Twentieth-Century Fox in which he played a Negro cavalry trooper who volunteers for an important mission. A short time later he moved into the business world as a marketing executive for Pepsi-Cola Company, then became linked with Main Bout, Inc., a sports promotion firm that eventually handled the fights of Muhammad (Cassius Clay) Ali. This association with the controversial Ali cast Brown as a strong civil-rights activist. But as the Ali bouts grew in controversy and were blocked out of arenas across the nation in 1966 because of the fighter's military draft status, Brown quietly signed for his second movie, "The Dirty Dozen."

The movie was filmed in London during the spring and summer of 1966 and became the stage on which Brown was abruptly to announce his retirement from football. Brown's plans originally called for his returning to the Browns for a tenth and final season before retiring. But the filming of "The Dirty Dozen" went overtime, delayed by rainy weather, and Brown startled the sports world and the Browns by serving notice that they would have to do without him for the 1966 season. What apparently solidified Brown's decision was Modell's announcement earlier that Brown would be fined for each day he failed to report to the Browns' training camp already in session in mid-July.

Upon completion of the movie, Brown returned to the United States and reaffirmed his retirement. He said his ambition

UPI
John Brewer (83) takes Eagles' Maxie Baughan out of Jim Brown's path.

94

now was to help members of his race gain economic equality. He formed the National Negro Industrial and Economic Union, enrolled more than 100 famous Negro sports figures, and opened offices throughout the country.

With the release of "The Dirty Dozen," in which he played a tough, racially conscious soldier who was one of 12 convicted murderers given the chance for redemption by being parachuted behind German lines during World War II, he became an instant movie star and hero to millions of Negroes. They flocked in unprecedented numbers to see his movies, quickly identifying with his rugged roles, typifying the black ethnic. His magnetism on the screen made him a sure-fire box-office attraction. He was promptly put under long-term contract. No other football player had made so successful and dramatic an impact as a movie star.

Whatever Jim Brown attempted to do, no matter what walk of life, he seemed to do it with a strong sense of reality. His attitude toward the many football records he set seems to bear that out.

"I think every record I've ever made will get wiped out, ultimately," he has said. "Always, you're going to have young guys coming along and improving. That's great, the way it needs to be, because that's progress, that's advancement. I never dwell on what I did; it's history now. I have a lot of pleasant memories of a game that was a good part of my life."

Year	Team	G.	RUSHES Att.	Yds.	Avg.	TDs	RECEPTIONS No.	Yds.	Avg.	TDs
1957	Clev.	12	202	942	4.7	9	16	55	3.4	1
1958	Clev.	12	257	1,527	5.9	17	16	138	8.6	1
1959	Clev.	12	290	1,329	4.6	14	24	190	7.9	0
1960	Clev.	12	215	1,257	5.8	9	19	204	10.7	2
1961	Clev.	14	305	1,408	4.6	8	46	459	10.0	2
1962	Clev.	14	230	996	4.3	13	47	517	11.0	5
1963	Clev.	14	291	1,863	6.4	12	24	268	11.2	3
1964	Clev.	14	280	1,446	5.2	7	36	340	9.4	2
1965	Clev.	14	289	1,544	5.3	17	34	328	9.6	4
Totals		118	2,359	12,312	5.2	106	262	2,499	9.5	20

Year	KICKOFF RETURNS No.	Yds.	Avg.	TDs	SCORING TDs	Pts.
1957	6	136	22.7	0	10	60
1958	3	74	24.7	0	18	108
1959	4	88	22.0	0	14	84
1960	14	300	21.4	0	11	66
1961	2	50	25.0	0	10	60
1962	0	0	0.0	0	18	108
1963	0	0	0.0	0	15	90
1964	0	0	0.0	0	9	54
1965	0	0	0.0	0	21	126
Totals	29	648	22.3	0	126	756

UPI
Sprints through opening as St. Louis Cardinal defenders try to box him in from both sides.

Gale Sayers

Gale Sayers
by William N. Wallace

Simply put, there are two species of running backs—the "hitter" and the "cutter." Jim Brown of the Cleveland Browns has been rated the best of the hitters and Gale Sayers of the Chicago Bears the best of the cutters.

The cutters begin back with Red Grange of the Bears in the late 1920's. Then there is a jump of 30 years to The King, Hugh McElhenny of the San Francisco 49ers, and on to Sayers, and, more currently, to O. J. Simpson of the Buffalo Bills and Larry Brown of the Washington Redskins.

The first great one, Red Grange, predictably had knee problems, which also plagued so many others who followed, including Sayers.

The cutters are those who change their routes to move away from the tacklers. They dodge and dart. The clichés are many

UPI

Stopped by Tommy Nobis of Falcons as Bears' blocking breaks down.

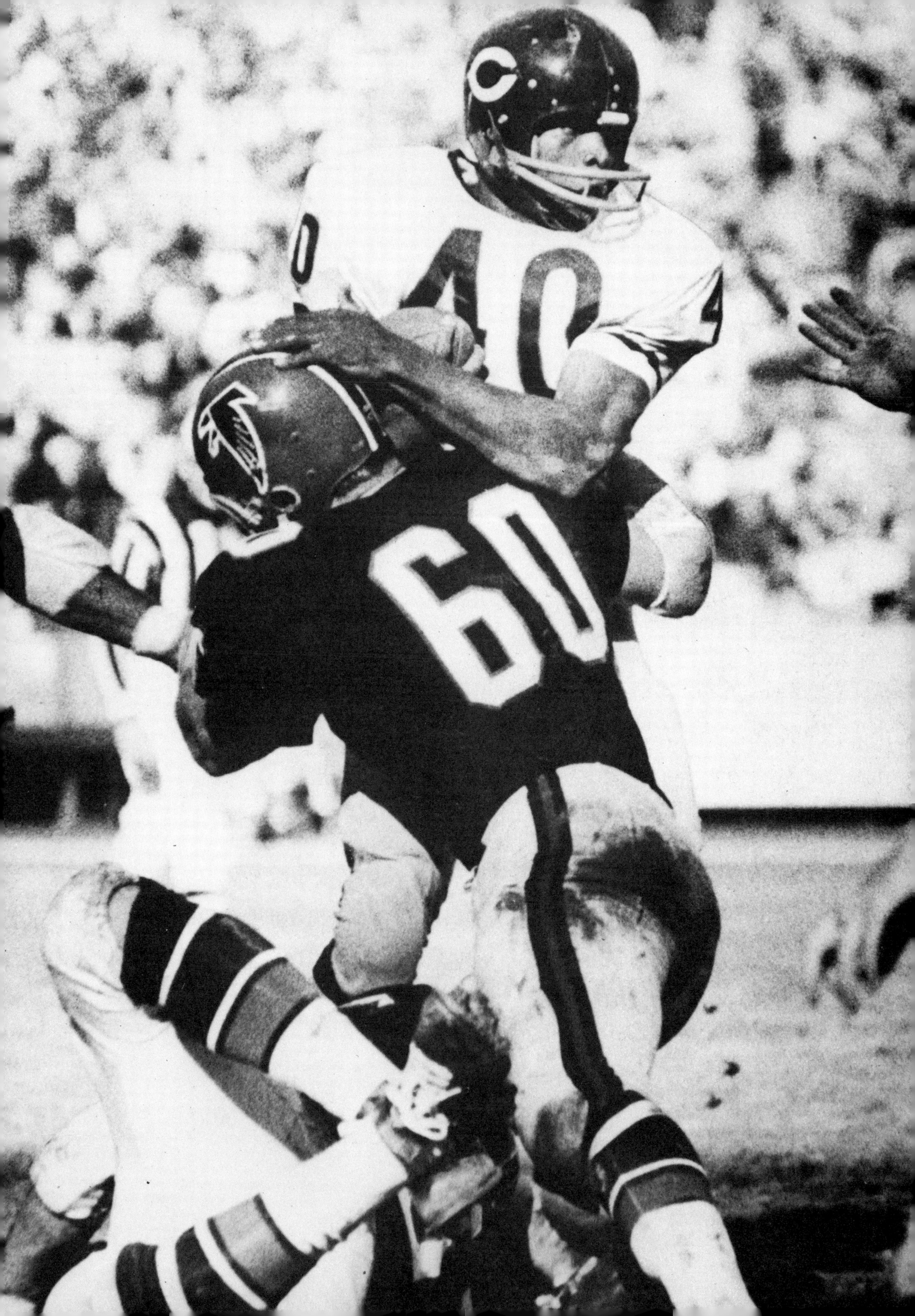

Gale Sayers running at full speed in the rain against the 49ers.

—swivel-hipped, give-'em-a-leg and take it away, fake him out of his jock. Their skill is one that can never be coached.

Jim Brown probably came as close as anyone to combining the two styles. He hit them when they were there and he also ran away from them. Basically, he belongs with the hitters, even though he disdained blocking. "I'm not paid to block," he said, and he was right.

The cutters operate largely on instinct. After watching himself on film one time, Sayers had no explanation of how he made a spectacular broken-field run. "I wasn't aware of what I was doing," he said about his swerves and cuts as he went upfield, always upfield.

But Gale did have techniques and he certainly was conscious of all the marvelous fakes he could put on the foe—head fakes, shoulder fakes, waist fakes.

George Halas has seen them all. He coached Grange, Bronko Nagurski, Norm Standlee, and Sayers, among others. So it is meaningful when Halas says that Gale Sayers was pro football's finest running back.

Sayers was not around very long, only four full seasons (1965, 1966, 1967 and 1969), before the inevitable knee injuries forced a premature retirement as the 1972 season was about to begin.

The first time it became apparent that a very special talent had arrived in the National Football League was in late November at Yankee Stadium when the Chicago Bears took on the New York Giants. The year was 1965, Sayers' rookie season, and this was the day he first gained over 100 yards from scrimmage. It was the ease with which he made 113 yards on only 13 carries that one remembers so well.

The Giants were nothing special that season, notably lacking on defense, but

Sayers made the New York linebackers appear to be statues. Gale scored on runs of 45 and 15 yards in an easy 35–14 victory and he struck terror in the hearts of the Giant special teams by merely lining up to receive the punts and kickoffs.

The Bears beat the Colts, who were very good, the next week as Sayers rushed for 118 yards. The following Sunday will never quite be forgotten on Chicago's North Side. The Bears beat the 49ers, 61–20, at Wrigley Field as Sayers scored six touchdowns to tie a league record shared by Ernie Nevers of the Chicago (now St. Louis) Cardinals and Dub Jones of the Browns.

He also set a single-game record by gaining 336 yards rushing, receiving and returning kicks. The first touchdown was an 80-yard pass play; the fourth a 50-yard run, and the sixth an 85-yard punt return. His 22 touchdowns for the season was another NFL record.

Chicago finished 1½ games behind the Packers and Colts for the Western Conference title and that was as close as the team came in Sayers' time to a playoff game or a championship. If the Bears had only had consistent quarterbacking or a decent defense, NFL history would have been different.

Consider 1969, Gale's last full season. The Bears were bad. They won only one game, but Sayers somehow gained 1,032 yards to lead the league in rushing. He was hard to catch.

Of course, the Kansas Comet had great balance. He had a long stride for a man of his size, 6 feet, about 200 pounds, and he ran low with his upper body out over his toes. But the uncanny bit about Sayers was the sideways business.

He would often interrupt his forward progress in heavy traffic with an effortless one-step glide 90 degrees left or right. Opponents swore this was so.

In the introduction to the Sayers' autobiography, *I Am Third,* Bill Cosby tells of watching a Pro Bowl game in Los Angeles from the sidelines as Sayers came around end with five defensive players waiting for him.

"I saw Gale Sayers split," wrote Cosby. "He just split in two. He threw the right side of his body one way and the left side of his body kept going. The defensive men didn't know who to catch."

Roosevelt Grier, the 300-pound tackle for the Rams, found Sayers coming at him, cutting back on a screen-pass play. "I hit him so hard," said Grier, "I thought my shoulder must have busted him in half. I heard the crowd roar, so I figured he must have fumbled. I started scrambling around, looking for the loose ball. But there was no ball, and Sayers was gone."

Gone 80 yards for a touchdown.

Sayers was a ghetto kid from Omaha, one of hundreds of dirt-poor black kids, naive and frightened, and therefore easy to be taken in by recruiters and exploiters. With virtually no tools, Sayers managed to survive and retire from sports relatively well-off. He was one in a 100, or one in 500.

His parents had an alcoholic history and the poverty ran deep. Sayers and his older brother shot sparrows to survive one winter. And mere survival was the name of the game, that and football.

Sayers was a tremendous high school football player and 100 colleges were out to recruit him. His academic credentials were slim, but no one cared. He was almost inarticulate and had a slight speech impediment. He read magazines, not books. He was withdrawn and suspicious, uncomfortable among strangers, especially white strangers who spoke well, had money and knew what to do in a restaurant or on an airplane. Sayers had to start from scratch. But he could run; oh, how he could run!

For a college he spurned Nebraska and took Kansas because the Jayhawk star,

Curtis McClinton, told him it was a good school for black athletes. Because of his decision to attend a rival Big Eight school, Sayers was roundly abused by many fans in his native state of Nebraska.

Sayers almost flunked out in his freshman year. Then he married the girl from Omaha he had been dating in high school, Linda, and her stability carried Gale through the academic hurdles the next three years. She worked and he studied when football permitted.

Jack Mitchell was the Kansas coach. He was popular and reasonably successful, although the Sayers teams never could beat Nebraska in 1962, 1963 or 1964. Gale played in every game, made all-America twice, and piled up plenty of yards.

When the time came for the pro draft in November, Sayers was ranked as one of the top three running backs of the country, along with Ken Willard of North Carolina and Tucker Frederickson of Auburn.

The two leagues, American and National, were in competition then and the prices were going up and up. Joe Namath, the celebrated $400,000 rookie quarterback from Alabama, was in that draft.

The Kansas City Chiefs wanted Sayers, and Don Klosterman, the chief scout, almost had the star from nearby Lawrence wrapped up.

The National Football League was running a "baby-sitting" operation at that time to counter the sometimes secret or early drafting arrangements of the younger league. Buddy Young, then on the staff of Commissioner Pete Rozelle, was Sayers' baby-sitter and they became strong friends.

The NFL aim was to tie up a player until

UPI
In his greatest one-game performance, Sayers shakes off 49ers' Kermit Alexander and races to one of the six touchdowns he tallied against San Francisco to equal an NFL scoring record during his rookie season.

the actual draft had taken place and he was assigned a team. Young could not tell Sayers which team would draft him, but kept Gale interested so that Kansas City would not sign him in advance of the NFL draft.

The Giants had first choice and took Frederickson. The 49ers came next and selected Willard. The third pick was Chicago's—for Gale. Sayers did not know anything about Chicago, but Young did. It was his home town. He sold Sayers on the Bears and Gale signed, four years for $25,000 a year plus a $50,000 bonus.

The Chiefs offered more, but it was too late. Sayers had made a deal.

"He came into pro football without an agent and he left the same way," said Young years later. "He negotiated all his contracts. He had a job his first year in pro football during the off season and he later became a stockbroker. He made a lot of money and he kept it all. When you consider his background, he did an awful lot for himself."

Sayers worked for Paine, Webber, Jackson & Curtis, the large brokerage house in Chicago. He was also a representative of Continental Airlines and the Aurora plastic-toy firm, and he wrote a sports column for the Chicago Daily News.

Sayers in 1965 was the runaway rookie of the year in the NFL, all league with Jim Brown at running back and a Pro Bowl performer. In his second season he led the NFL in yards-gained rushing. He thought he had a slump in 1967, although no one else did.

Then, in the ninth game of the 1968 season, he went down, hit by the San Francisco 49ers' cornerback, Kermit Alexander,

UPI
Gale Sayers' explosive charge sends Earsall Mackbee of Vikings (46) reeling backward.

UPI
Swift Sayers bursts through St. Louis Cardinals for a 30-yard gain.

UPI
Gale Sayers flies over teammate and looks for daylight against Browns.

with a rolling low shoulder block. Ligaments were torn in the right knee.

Following surgery, Sayers worked very hard on a recovery program and came all the way back for a brilliant season in 1969.

The New York sportswriters awarded Sayers the comeback-of-the-year award for his courage, and at their banquet in May, 1970, Sayers passed the award along to his friend, Brian Piccolo, who was dying of cancer.

The close Sayers-Piccolo relationship was the basis of a later fictionalized television movie that had great vogue, "Brian's Song."

Their relationship began slowly when both were rookies, Sayers the inhibited star whose favorite response was, "Nope," Piccolo the ebullient, gregarious substitute to whom no one paid much regard.

They later became roommates on road trips and at training camp at a time when such black-white friendships were less than common. Piccolo was especially valuable in helping Sayers through the first knee-surgery experience which was so traumatic to Gale.

Sayers injured his other knee in training camp in 1970 and underwent surgery again in October. An attempted return in 1971 failed, and Sayers retired following a miserable exhibition-game effort in 1972 when he fumbled on two of three carries, setting up two St. Louis touchdowns.

It was all over, but by Sayers' choice. He could have stayed on the roster to collect his $70,000 salary. He might have tried to make it back as a receiver, so his knees would not take such a beating.

"It was his pride," said his friend, Young. "He was going to make it as a running back or not at all. He never believed in excuses."

			RUSHES				RECEPTIONS			
Year	Team	G.	Att.	Yds.	Avg.	TDs	No.	Yds.	Avg.	TDs
1965	Chicago	14	166	867	5.2	14	29	507	17.5	6
1966	Chicago	14	229	1,231	5.4	8	34	447	13.1	2
1967	Chicago	13	186	880	4.7	7	16	126	7.9	1
1968	Chicago	9	138	856	6.2	2	15	117	7.8	0
1969	Chicago	14	236	1,032	4.4	8	17	116	6.8	0
1970	Chicago	2	23	52	2.3	0	1	−6	−6.0	0
1971	Chicago	2	13	38	2.9	0	0	0	0.0	0
Totals		68	991	4,956	5.0	39	112	1,307	11.7	9

	PUNT RETURNS				KICKOFF RETURNS				SCORING	
Year	No.	Yds.	Avg.	TDs	No.	Yds.	Avg.	TDs	TDs	Pts.
1965	16	238	14.9	1	21	660	31.4	1	22	132
1966	6	44	7.3	0	23	718	31.2	2	12	72
1967	3	80	26.7	1	16	603	37.7	3	12	72
1968	2	29	14.5	0	17	461	27.1	0	2	12
1969	0	0	0.0	0	14	339	24.2	0	8	48
1970	0	0	0.0	0	0	0	0.0	0	0	0
1971	0	0	0.0	0	0	0	0.0	0	0	0
Totals	27	391	14.5	2	91	2,781	30.6	6	56	336

In full motion with guard John Demarie blocking up front against Pittsburgh Steelers.

Leroy Kelly

Leroy Kelly
by Marty Ralbovsky

When the magnificent Jim Brown decided to forget about football in the summer of 1966, many people predicted disaster for the Cleveland Browns. The list did not include William ("Dub") Jones, who at that time was the Cleveland backfield coach. In fact, Dub Jones had tagged Leroy Kelly as a future star almost six months before Jim Brown's decision to give his all to the film set.

"I'd be willing to match Leroy's potential with any of the much-publicized backs coming out of college," Jones declared at the time. "He's way above average. In fact, he eventually may move in with the super players. Leroy is a perfectly proportioned 205 pounds. He has a fine sense of timing. He sort of leads would-be tacklers into a trap and then bursts away. Balance is another of his assets. He doesn't get knocked

UPI

Vaults into end zone for deciding score against Bengals as Al Beauchamp and Bill Bergey (right) fail to push him back.

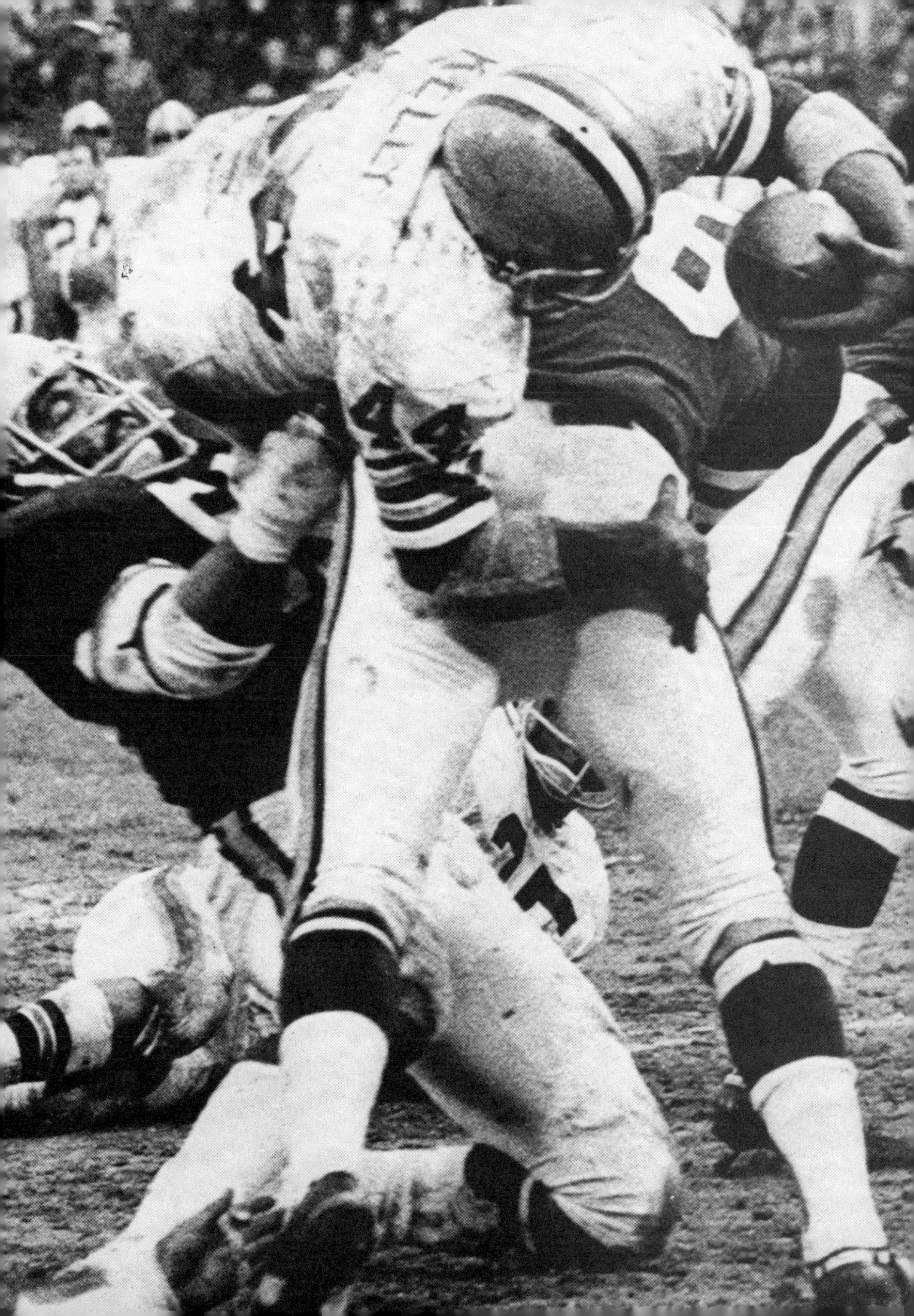

down easily." Dub Jones, a tremendous performer himself while with the Browns in the early 1950's, proved to be a prophet.

Quiet Leroy Kelly teamed with Ernie Green, Jim Brown's old running mate, in 1966 and he gained 1,141 yards. In the next two years he proceeded to win back-to-back rushing titles in the National Football League. The former Philadelphia high school star, who had his first real recognition at Morgan State College in Baltimore, has a 4.9-yard average for his career. He has run for 1,000 yards three times in a season and undoubtedly would have made it two other times except for injuries.

Ernie Green, having performed in the same backfield with both Brown and Kelly, said: "Leroy is like a cat. So was Jim, only a bigger cat. It's difficult to knock a cat off his feet. Kelly is agile and has balance. As far as attitude goes, there is seriousness about his play. Both he and Brown are no-nonsense runners. When they go out on the field, they mean business.

"Leroy doesn't have Jim's strength, so he has to compensate in other ways. Jim broke tackles, Kelly has to move about more, slide around, give head and shoulder fakes, and sidestep to get around tacklers."

Kelly has also shown another asset—durability. Until a muscle pull in 1970, he never failed to answer a whistle since winning the starting job. Asked about that durability, he said: "A lot of it certainly is luck. Good physical condition helps, of course. Jim, for instance, liked to do a lot of running before the start of a game. I have my own style. I just like to break a sweat."

Kelly also has shown a knack for applying the second effort, and when to accept the inevitable and go down. "I see runners fight long after it's obvious they aren't going to get away, even for a couple of yards," he said. "There is a time to give that second effort that can be so important on occasions. There also is a time to find a spot, preferably a soft one, and go down. You used to read a lot about Jim Taylor being a punishing runner. That could be the reason he received so many punishing tackles. I guess it's instinct. Sometimes you know when to fight on, and sometimes you know when to go down."

Leroy Kelly was recommended to the Browns by Buddy Young, after the Baltimore Colts turned him down. Kelly is a quiet, but strong-minded, young man; he showed the latter side of his character after the 1966 season when he demanded a sizable raise. He rejected an increase of about $12,000 and instead played out his option. It was a daring gamble, but it paid off in March of 1968 when Art Modell, the Cleveland owner, rewarded him with a lucrative four-year contract.

Leroy admits that he still sometimes wonders how he had the nerve to go through the season without being signed. "It was taking a big chance. I had the good fortune to stay healthy."

All the money, and some travel, have made more of an extrovert out of Kelly. He's still pretty much a steak and chicken man at dinner, but his taste in clothes, cars and music have widened with his affluence. *Esquire* magazine tapped him as one of the ten best-dressed young men in America. And his wardrobe has expanded considerably since that occasion.

Boyd's of Philadelphia produces most of his clothes. He purchases suits three at a time, and has lost count of the number hanging in the closets of his bachelor apartment in one of Cleveland's eastern suburbs.

Stacks of records and his record player are prominent in the living room. "I like rock more than classical," he said, "but I go for all types of music." He also enjoys fishing and golf. And that's how he spends most of his time during the off-season. "Fishing is the thing that really relaxes me.

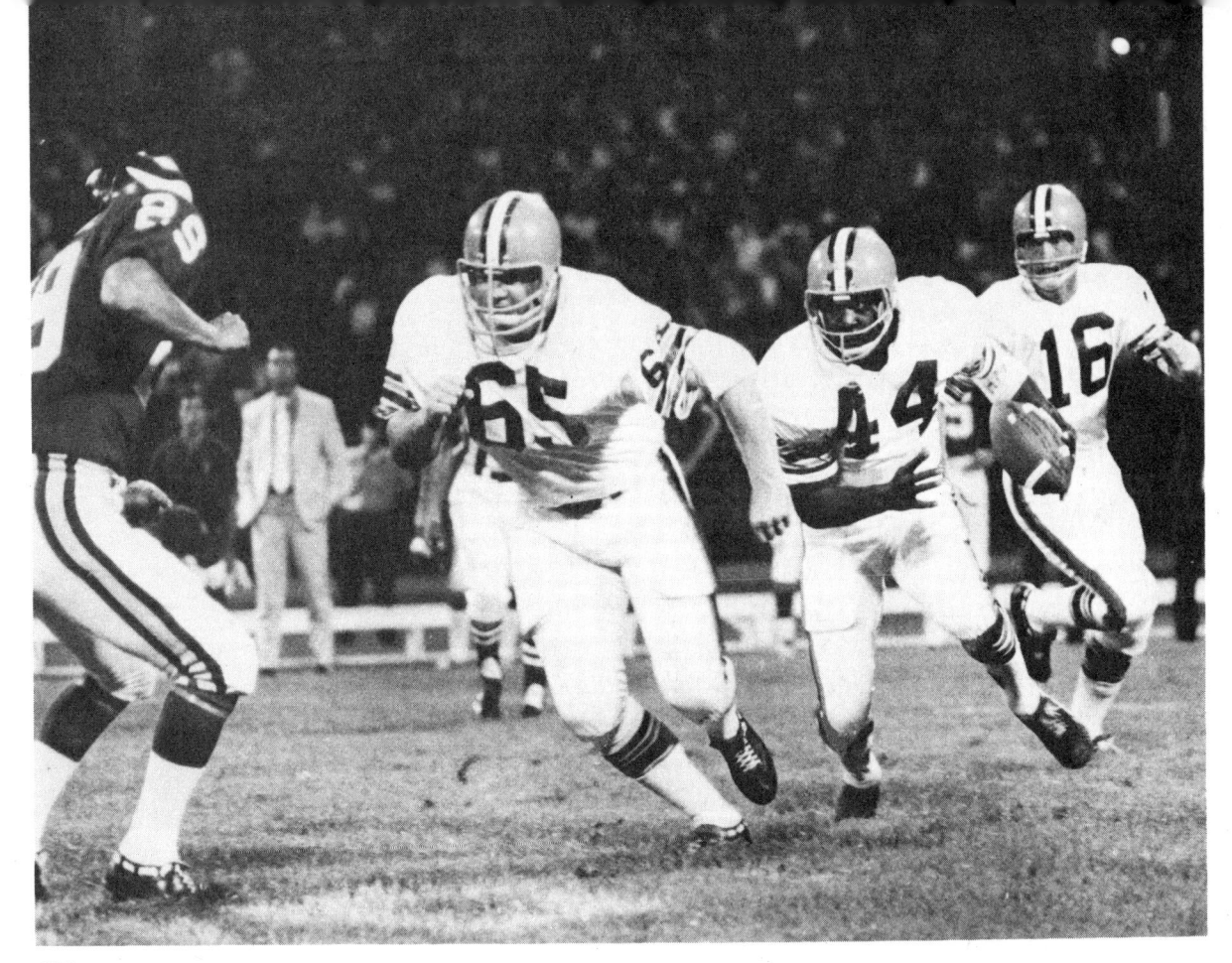

After taking hand-off from Bill Nelson (16), Kelly goes for first down against Vikings as John Demarie (65) gets set to check Karl Kassulke (29).

I always go just before the start of camp, either into Canada or to some other place, where the fishing is good. I've been a fisherman ever since I was 11 or 12 years old. Back in Philadelphia we first used to go for sunfish. Later we went deep-sea fishing off New Jersey." Golf is a more recent pastime, but Kelly now shoots in the low 80's much of the time.

* * *

Leroy Kelly is the second youngest child of a large family. His mother is a worrier; she worries about Leroy getting hurt. She was not unhappy when her youngest son, Harold, decided to take a $7,500 bonus from the Minnesota Twins, rather than accept a football scholarship. "I tried to talk Harold into following me at Morgan State," Leroy said, "but he wanted to get started in baseball." Harold, an outfielder who also is called Pat, plays for the Kansas City Royals.

Kelly's father was a mechanic with the G. & W. H. Corson Company, a lime factory, and he once played semi-pro baseball himself. The family grew up in the upper section of North Philadelphia known as Nicetown, now predominantly a black neighborhood. Fortunately, they lived next to Fern Hill Park, where the Kelly Boys had plenty of room to play. All the Kelly boys played football, baseball, and basketball at Simon Graetz High School.

"For four straight years we had a Kelly at quarterback," said the coach at Simon Graetz, Louis De Vicaris. "Leroy was the best football player I ever coached."

At Simon Graetz, Leroy was the highest scorer in the Public League and received the most votes for the All-Public team. "He did everything for us," recalled De Vicaris. "He kicked off, punted, received punts and, on defense, he played the toughest spot, middle linebacker, in the 7-diamond. He made 50 percent of the tackles.

"On offense he was our T-quarterback. In our setup, the quarterback did plenty of running. We used lots of rollouts and slants. He had a great change-of-pace. Once he got past the line of scrimmage, it was a good bet he'd score. Once we had fourth-and-12 on the two-yard line. It was a close game and we gambled on a run. Leroy went 98 yards for the score and we broke the other team's back.

"Though he was very, very quiet, he was a real leader here," said De Vicaris. "He didn't smoke, never missed a practice, always reported on time, and he ran hard even when it would have been okay for him to jog. He was a leader by example, an aggressive, competitive type who would rap a teammate on the helmet or kick him in the pants if he didn't put out. I wish we had some leaders like him around now."

When graduation time approached, De Vicaris sent letters to several black colleges extolling Leroy's ability. Leroy, a fine shortstop, had considered baseball as a career, but he preferred a college education. He majored in auto mechanics in high school and that made it difficult for him to follow up feelers from Temple and Michigan State. But Morgan State suited Leroy fine, since Baltimore is close to Philadelphia, and he had never been away from home before.

Like De Vicaris at Graetz High School, Coach Banks at Morgan State discovered Leroy could do everything on offense: block, run, catch passes. As good as Leroy was, though, Banks said, "I don't think we got one-third of his full potential. Why, I don't know. Seemingly, he has more motivation now. The fact that he's getting a chance with the pros may be the added incentive, or that he's trying to fill the shoes of Jim Brown."

* * *

Filling Jim Brown's shoes was no easy chore. Once, in a game against the Green Bay Packers, Green Bay's defensive end, Willie Davis, went to work on the inexperienced Leroy. "Willie started with the first play," Ernie Green revealed. "He said all sorts of mean things to Leroy, like, 'Leroy,

UPI
Leroy Kelly is pursued by Dave Robinson (89) and Ray Nitschke of Packers.

you're not going to get anything today,' or, 'Every time you run, we'll break your neck.' I could see Leroy was bothered. He had heard fine things about Willie Davis and he couldn't understand it. Leroy became even more quiet than usual. I'd been through it before, so I was able to explain it to him. I said, 'They're just trying to upset you. It's a compliment. Pay no attentention to them.' He responded quickly."

The success of Kelly taught pro football a lesson, Dub Jones believed. "He has brought about the realization that you don't need big running backs to have a strong ground attack. Until him, there had been the strong feeling it was important to have size in the backfield. Kelly has shown you never can sacrifice quickness and co-ordination for size."

Four games after replacing Brown, Cleveland's owner, Art Modell, called Kelly into his office and surprised him with a new contract calling for a substantial increase. "The kid," recalled Modell, "was overcome with emotion." When Leroy recovered, he allowed himself the first real luxury of his life. He replaced his Chevelle with a new Cadillac.

Although Leroy is much less communicative than the Jim Brown he replaced, he communicated his displeasure to a Steeler once who had roughed him up. Leroy kicked him. Naturally, he was promptly awarded a 15-yard penalty. "I lost my head slightly in the heat of battle," he said. "Something like that shouldn't happen."

Except for running into a couple of "clothes-lines" (extended arms that catch a potential receiver in the windpipe), Leroy hasn't found pro football particularly rough. "I've only been hurt twice in football," he said. "I had a charley horse once in college and a muscle pull when I first joined the Browns."

Leroy has no fear of getting hurt. "My mother worries enough for the whole

Leroy Kelly high-stepping toward touchdown.

family," he said. And Mrs. Kelly has had plenty of practice worrying. She has four football-playing sons among her children. She never went to see them play, and even now, when the family travels from Philadelphia to Pittsburgh for Browns' games there, Mrs. Kelly stays home. She has mustered sufficient courage to watch a few of the Browns' games on TV a couple times, however.

* * *

Leroy Kelly remembers his days at Morgan State fondly. "Those were good days," he said. "The Colts used to come over to help out all the time. Big Daddy Lipscomb, Lenny Moore, and Buddy Young. He [Buddy Young] taught me the most im-

Kelly runs by Oilers at scrimmage line.

portant things I know about running—how to keep your eyes open after you get through the line and search for an avenue of escape. He taught me to keep my balance, and to keep my speed under control, and to open up when I've spotted the opening."

Down at Morgan State, people will tell you without hesitation that Leroy Kelly was the best football player the school has ever had. But, incredibly, he wasn't even going to get drafted by the pros until Coach Banks went to bat for him. Most pro scouts apparently thought that, at 200 pounds, he wasn't big enough to run in their league, and since he wasn't playing in a major conference there were no glowing reports of his activities in the sports sections.

Coach Banks called Buddy Young into the case. "Buddy," Banks said, "come to a couple of our games. Study Leroy and make a report on him. If you think he's good enough to play, let somebody up there know, because I'm afraid they're gonna pass him by."

Young agreed to do it. After studying Kelly in two games, he was so impressed he contacted the Browns and told them he was as good as any college halfback in the country. Paul Bixler, the Browns' talent scout, went to Baltimore to see Kelly play, and he was impressed, too.

What happened, according to Bixler, was this: "We needed a running back, and the men we wanted were gone by the time our first few turns came around. When it came down to the eighth round, I decided the best running back left was Kelly. So we took him."

Bixler made an offer. "It wasn't too much, and I told him I'd think it over," recalled Kelly. The New York Jets were also interested in Kelly. But the Cleveland offer went up and he signed. Kelly received a bonus of approximately $7,500 and a salary of $10,000.

"One thing," said Leroy when the deal was made, "I'd like a small advance on my salary. My brother just got a bonus from the Minnesota Twins and we both want to put some money together for a down payment on a new home for our parents." Kelly got the advance and, with Harold, made the initial payment on a house in Germantown, where the family now lives.

Blanton Collier, the Cleveland coach, invited Leroy to the "Spring Look" in Cleveland, where rookies go through speed tests, pass-catching, and other agility maneuvers while coaches evaluate them. "I was first impressed by his general ability," Collier recalled. "A lot of our people thought of him as a defensive man and punter. He thought of himself in that role. But after watching him move, I felt he had the ability to run with the ball. Trouble was, he weighed about 188."

"I wish you were bigger," Collier told him.

"I'll be bigger when I come back," promised Leroy, and he reported to camp in July, 1964, weighing 200. But in an effort to put on weight, he exercised at a minimum before reporting. As a result, he pulled a hamstring muscle during the fourth day in camp. The injury, and the fact that the champion Browns were getting ready to play the College All-Stars and therefore had little time for rookies, caused Kelly to lose ground in the learning program. When he healed, he played on the specialty teams.

The following year, Collier asked Leroy to report a week early for a crash classroom series to make up for lost time. "He learned fast," said Collier, "but we had a winning combination and we didn't want to break it up." So again Kelly stayed with the specialty units.

Then, in July, 1966, Jim Brown retired and Kelly stepped in and surprised almost everyone. "Frankly," says Paul Bixler, "I recommended him because I thought he was good. But he's much better than I judged him. I didn't think he'd be this great."

Leroy makes Cleveland his year-round home. He has become active in the Negro Industrial and Economic Union, headed by Jim Brown.

Being a "celebrity," Leroy is in demand for public appearances. The Quiet Man says, "I don't mind too much. I'm always trying to get a couple of jokes together." But mainly, Leroy Kelly intends to continue letting his feet—and feats—do the talking for him.

Year	Team	G.	RUSHES Att.	Yds.	Avg.	TDs	RECEPTIONS No.	Yds.	Avg.	TDs
1964	Clev.	14	6	12	2.0	0	0	0	0.0	0
1965	Clev.	13	37	139	3.8	0	9	122	13.6	0
1966	Clev.	14	209	1,141	5.5	15	32	366	11.4	1
1967	Clev.	14	235	1,205	5.1	11	20	282	14.1	2
1968	Clev.	14	248	1,239	5.0	16	22	297	13.5	4
1969	Clev.	13	196	817	4.2	9	20	267	13.4	1
1970	Clev.	13	206	656	3.2	6	24	311	13.0	2
1971	Clev.	14	234	865	3.7	10	25	252	10.1	2
1972	Clev.	14	224	811	3.6	4	23	204	8.9	1
Totals		123	1,595	6,885	4.3	71	175	2,101	12.0	13

Year	PUNT RETURNS No.	Yds.	Avg.	TDs	KICKOFF RETURNS No.	Yds.	Avg.	TDs	SCORING TDs	Pts.
1964	9	171	19.0	1	24	582	24.3	0	1	6
1965	17	265	15.6	2	24	621	25.9	0	2	12
1966	13	104	8.0	0	19	403	21.2	0	16	96
1967	9	59	6.6	0	5	131	26.2	0	13	78
1968	1	9	9.0	0	1	10	10.0	0	20	120
1969	7	28	4.0	0	2	26	13.0	0	10	60
1970	2	15	7.5	0	0	0	0.0	0	8	48
1971	30	292	9.7	0	1	11	11.0	0	12	72
1972	5	40	8.0	0	0	0	0.0	0	5	30
Totals	93	983	10.6	3	76	1,784	23.5	0	87	522

Accelerates as he sweeps right end against Patriots with George Goeddeke as blocker.

Floyd Little

Floyd Little
by Parton Keese

The rain poured down on Shea Stadium that December day in 1967. The Denver Broncos' rookie back, Floyd Little, gathered in a punt from the New York Jets on his own 28-yard line. Slithering through puddles, mud, and soggy players, he persevered and traveled 72 yards to the goal line. It proved to be the only time an American Football League player that year returned a punt all the way for a touchdown. On the next play, Little broke his left clavicle, and so his first pro season was over.

Just off the Syracuse University campus, hip-pad deep in press clippings, the first three-time all-American since Doak Walker, a halfback who had exploded on the country's football consciousness by scoring five touchdowns against Kansas as a sophomore, Little's first professional year

UPI

Uses right arm attempting to spin away for extra yardage as Browns' Dale Lindsey (51) reaches for him and ball.

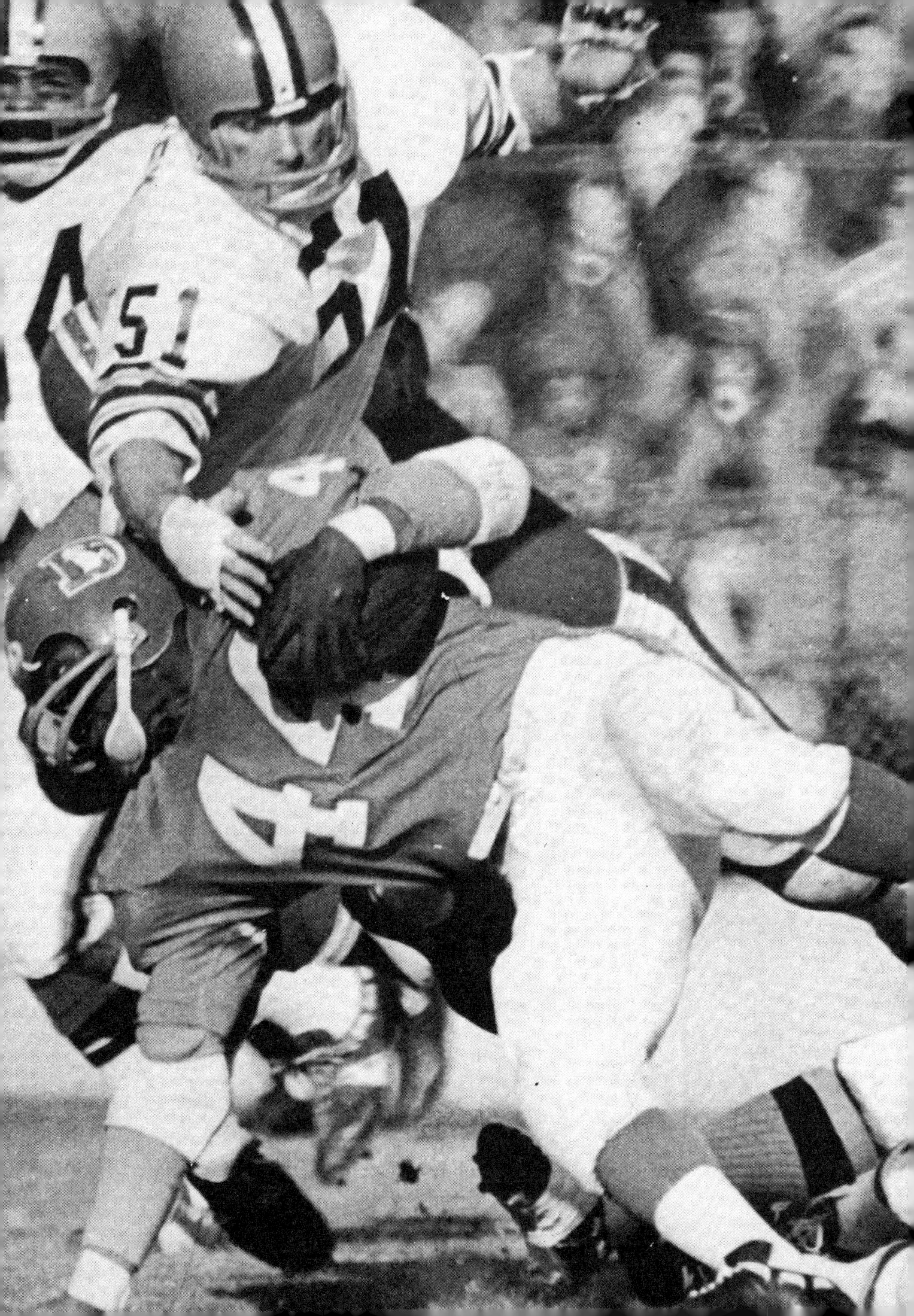
51

had not been quite the way many thought it would be.

But fate has a way of making up for some people, and Little would go on to lead the AFL three times in rushing, become the only player in league history to rank in the top 10 in kickoff and punt returns, as well as rushing, and be called by the man at Syracuse who had coached Jim Brown, Ernie Davis, Jim Nance, and Larry Csonka "the greatest running back he had ever seen."

Floyd first had to learn to overcome adversity. In his initial professional year, the player who set virtually every Syracuse rushing record, who scored in 22 of his 30 college games, who had a total offense of almost 5,000 yards, was still struggling to get over the 2-yard-per-carry average.

When he didn't achieve his first touchdown as a professional until his 11th game, when his longest run from scrimmage all year was just 14 yards, and when at one point he found himself on the bench, Little's morale dropped, his weight fell from 196 pounds to 180, and he became so depressed he contemplated quitting.

Two special visits turned the season—and Little's pro career—around. The first was to a doctor who discovered an iron deficiency and put him on a corrective diet. In no time his weight jumped back to normal. The second visit was to Lou Saban, his Denver coach, which lasted only 20 minutes but changed his whole attitude.

"Floyd wanted so badly to contribute to the ball club," Saban said. "He felt that, due to circumstances, it was up to him to produce more than anyone else. When it didn't come, it was mental torture."

When Saban told him he couldn't expect to score a touchdown every time, that the

UPI
Little unable to avoid waist-high tackle by Houston Oiler during 1972 game.

Broncos' fate didn't rest entirely on his shoulders, Floyd finally stopped worrying, and he was restored to the starting team.

"Those four weeks were the worst of my life," he recalls emotionally. "It was just anxiety. I could feel every play, whether I was in there or not."

Some people had begun to wonder, though, if he wasn't just another highly touted, high-priced pro failure. But Little began to prove he wasn't in the second half of that season. One Sunday he gained 126 yards rushing against Miami. The next Sunday he rushed for a team record of 147 yards against Boston. On one play, he took a pitchout, reversed his field, and raced 55 yards to score. A week later he returned a kickoff 89 yards against Oakland. The following week he returned a punt 67 yards against Houston in the Astrodome.

He was so adept at returning punts that he became the first rookie in the league to capture season honors in that category with a 16.9-yard average. He also finished third-best in kickoff runbacks.

Teammates were quick to see the changes in Little, too. "At first, Floyd seemed all uptight, alone and tense," said one, "but he started to loosen up, and now he's really rolling." Dave Costa, the defensive captain, had another explanation: "Floyd's teammates, when he broke in, were as green as he was, so he had no one to turn to for help. He just had to find himself through a lot of tough games."

"One of the things you learn as a pro," Little says, "is that the other guys are good, too, and they're gonna beat you on some plays. You've got to just forget it and fight back on the next play. You've got to take the long view of the season. You have to psych yourself to do your best, no matter what. That's what you're being paid for. This is a business. I still enjoy the game, but I approach it as a pro now, not as a rah-rah amateur."

With this revitalized thinking, Floyd Little went on to lead the AFC three times in rushing, while in 1971 he led the NFL with 1,133 yards, scoring a half-dozen touchdowns. With Floyd leading the way, the Broncos seemed to grow more sure of themselves, too. Little became Denver's offensive captain, pointed out by his coach as one of the team's leaders, and acknowledged by his peers as one of the game's outstanding runners.

No bruiser as a running back—he's only 5-feet-10 inches tall and 196 pounds—it has usually been a struggle for Floyd. In 1970 he played the last two games of the season with a cracked bone in his back. Nevertheless, his speed and power carried him to the conference rushing championship with 901 yards.

Injuries were nothing new to him, either. As a pro, he has suffered a cracked collarbone, a wrenched back, a strained sternum, a sprained ankle, and a severely lacerated finger, along with a bad spell of the flu, not to mention that iron deficiency in his blood.

One of Little's weapons against a letdown has been his attitude. "You've got to make a distinction between pain and injury," Floyd said. "I wouldn't play more than one game a year—the first one—if I let pain keep me out. Trouble is, a lot of guys coming up don't know the difference between hurting and being hurt."

An early-season incident illustrates this point graphically. Against San Diego one year Little had played only one quarter. He was crushed between a couple of big tackles and suffered deep bruises on both thighs. He had to come out. When Denver returned home, Little had to be taken off the plane in a wheelchair, and he spent the night in a hospital. The following Sunday he carried 21 times for 96 yards against Kansas City and caught a touchdown pass on the first offensive play of the game.

That Floyd is tough and plays hard is

common knowledge. But he even practices hard. One time, catching a pass in practice, he dented a metal barrier 10 yards from the sidelines. At home he once cracked a wall while recreating a play for friends. One of his most treasured football memories is the time he and his former Syracuse running mate, 240-pound Jim Nance, would go one-on-one against each other in a practice game.

"I used to kid him I'd knock him into the bleachers if I ever got the chance," Floyd recalled. "In this game, I broke loose with only him between me and the goal line. I could have faked him easily. Instead, I drove right into him. Oh, my! We both went 10 yards straight up. It was beautiful."

The Broncos' trainer remarked on Little's ability to bounce back: "Floyd is the type of athlete who could survive being run over by a train and then say, 'I'm not doing too well right now, but I'll be ready by Sunday.'"

The ailments that have plagued him on the playing field are varied and remarkable. However, the interesting aspect of Little's physique is that he is pronouncedly bowlegged, a characteristic that he says has saved him from destruction.

"I'm the most bowlegged runner you ever saw," he points out, "maybe the most bowlegged of whoever played the game. Some guy comes in and gives me a pop on the side of my leg and my knee just straightens up into a normal position, instead of getting all banged-up. Straighten me out and I'm a good 6-feet-2."

"But I did have a hard couple of years," Floyd said of his early pro career. "I guess I should have expected that. Nothing ever came easy to me in my life."

* * *

Born on July 4, 1942, in Waterbury, Connecticut, Floyd Douglas Little was 6 years old when his father died of cancer. His mother was left to raise six children on $3,200 a year from welfare, living in a poor black section of town.

Floyd was a homely, nervous child, and for a long time would venture out into the world only when he could hang onto an older sister's hand. Once he grew hysterical when separated from her. The other children called him "Cheetah" and mocked him. He was so sensitive that when he once mispronounced a word in the third grade and others laughed at him, he refused to read aloud in school for years afterward.

His mother moved her family to New Haven when Floyd was 13, settling in another ghetto. In one house in which they lived there were 26 children on three floors. It seemed all of them were destined to remain in the poverty cycle, but Floyd found hope in sports.

He was a fast, agile youngster, good at all kinds of athletic games, though he seldom practiced because he had to spend time as a shoeshine boy. Every dollar counted in the Little family. At Hillhouse High School he established himself as a football prospect. Football was about all he learned there, though. Once he applied for a job as a janitor, but was rejected because he was unable to fill out the application blank properly.

Receiving a football scholarship to Bordentown Military Academy in New Jersey, Floyd played brilliantly and learned to study. Colleges began to seek him, and because Ernie Davis had been his idol, he chose Syracuse—and by a sad coincidence —on the same day that Davis died of leukemia. Little added glory to the same No. 44 that Davis and Jim Brown wore there by breaking all of their records. He gained 2,704 yards rushing and totaled nearly 5,000 yards in all offensive categories as a spectacular breakaway runner.

Following the frustrations of his rookie year as the Broncos' No. 1 draft pick and the injuries that hampered him early the next season, Little began to prove his worth. Almost from nowhere, his statistics shot upward like a rocket. He moved from 381 yards gained in his rookie year to 584 yards the second year, and then to 729. In 1970 he hit 901 yards, while in 1971 he ran for 1,133 yards, breaking the Broncos' all-time record and leading the National Football League. The feat not only represented Floyd's top goal, it proved to everyone he had arrived as a superstar.

Since Denver was notorious for its lack of huge linemen, Little's exploits are all the more extraordinary. As for himself, no longer a tongue-tied schoolboy, Floyd traced his success to speed, or rather a variation of speed, as it is commonly acknowledged.

"Some are faster," he noted, "but I can

UPI
No hole opens up against Raiders, so Little climbs over pile of players.

run as fast sideways as I can straight ahead, which few can. I can accelerate fast and shift speeds smoothly. I'm small, but that helps me to hide. I'm hard to spot behind big linemen. Also, it's hard to get down to my legs, which is the only place to bring me down.

"I'm strong, too. I have good balance and I make good use of my arms, which I swing to break tackles. I run skittering, like a mouse eluding a cat. I can't explain my moves. I don't think any good runner can. I can't copy anyone. I don't know what I'm doing until I do it. Then I can never repeat it. It's some kind of instinct."

Don Horn hands off to Floyd Little who watches how blocking patterns will develop as he runs.

"Fluid" is the word his opponents use for Little—running hard, but with liquid motion, breaking a hard tackle to get extra yards or reaching out to catch a long pass on his fingertips and pivoting away from two defenders to get more yards on another play.

The one thing that turns Floyd into even more of a demon is an interception on a pass play. Once when he made a vicious tackle after the pass intended for him was picked off, he said: "I hate the interceptions, but I love those tackles. I love contact. I'd rather play defense than offense. Why should I be the one taking the raps? I'd rather be running those other cats down and tearing their heads off."

Hunter Enis, who coached him at Denver, said, "Little is a very strong guy, probably one of the strongest we've got. He has great balance, great quickness, and great change of pace. Floyd has that quality that tells you something good is going to happen when he gets the ball."

Though constructed like a massive pair of pliers, Little knows the score, too. He leads his ball club with his tongue as well as his body, and he gives plenty of credit to his blockers.

"Look, I know what the stat sheet says. What it doesn't say is that a linebacker, a defensive end, and a halfback are after me every play—before the ball even moves. I'm not Joe Superback. Nobody can run through that stack without help."

But Little's leadership isn't restricted to sideline psychology. Take, for instance, the game against the Jets where the Broncos had managed but six plays from scrimmage the first quarter while the Jets were recording 13 points. When New York was forced to punt from its end zone, Bill Thompson, a rookie cornerback, stood alongside Little to receive the ball. "Floyd yelled over to me," Thompson said, " 'We need a big play, Bill. They've got to have a lift.' "

Stepping in front of Thompson at Denver's 47-yard line, Little fielded the punt and returned it to the Jets' 1 before Mike Battle caught him. He then scored on the next play.

"I've never seen a look of such pure determination on a man's face before," an awed Bronco tackle said of the punt return. "You just *knew* he was going all the way, and you knew things were going to be all right."

So dedicated and intense is Little that he startled the new-breed players during an exhibition game with the Baltimore Colts. A Denver punt receiver was hurt and the new coaching staff looked hurriedly around for a quick solution to something that had caught them unprepared.

"I'll take over," said Little, grabbing his helmet and running out on the field. He volunteered, even though he was now the biggest star on the team. But he instantly showed why he was the biggest star by running back the kick for 88 yards and a touchdown.

What was Little's biggest thrill as a player? He says it came in 1968, ironically after he had fumbled in the closing minutes, with Denver nursing a 31–29 lead over Buffalo. George Saimes recovered and ran the ball back 27 yards to the Denver 10, where the Bills kicked a field goal to go ahead, 32–31, and apparently cinch a victory with only seconds left.

Little begged the Denver quarterback, Marlin Briscoe, to throw the ball to him after the ensuing kickoff. "I told him, 'You've got to let me make it up.' When he threw it, I knew I was going to catch it. I had to catch it. That's all there was to it. I didn't care who was there, I was going to get it."

He did, 59 yards downfield, and close enough to allow Denver to get a field goal and the victory.

Extraordinary afield, Little incorporates the same kind of philosophy in life. "I choose not to be an ordinary man," he once quoted as his motto, "because it is my right to be uncommon—if I can."

Year	Team	G.	RUSHES Att.	Yds.	Avg.	TDs	RECEPTIONS No.	Yds.	Avg.	TDs
1967	Denver	13	130	381	2.9	1	7	11	1.6	0
1968	Denver	11	158	584	3.7	3	19	331	17.4	1
1969	Denver	9	146	729	5.0	6	19	218	11.5	1
1970	Denver	14	209	901	4.3	3	17	161	9.5	0
1971	Denver	14	284	1,133	4.0	6	26	255	9.8	0
1972	Denver	14	216	859	4.0	9	28	367	13.1	4
Totals		75	1,143	4,587	4.0	28	116	1,343	11.6	6

Year	PUNT RETURNS No.	Yds.	Avg.	TDs	KICKOFF RETURNS No.	Yds.	Avg.	TDs	SCORING TDs	Pts.
1967	16	270	16.9	1	35	942	26.9	0	2	12
1968	24	261	10.9	1	26	649	25.0	0	5	30
1969	6	70	11.7	0	3	81	27.0	0	7	42
1970	22	187	8.5	0	6	126	21.0	0	3	18
1971	0	0	0.0	0	7	199	28.4	0	6	36
1972	8	64	8.0	0	3	48	16.0	0	13	78
Totals	76	852	11.2	2	80	2,045	25.6	0	36	216

UPI

Throws off Cardinal tackler and gets heads-up block from Dolphin teammate during 1972 game.

Larry Csonka

Larry Csonka

by Marty Ralbovsky

In an astoundingly short span of six years, the Miami Dolphins traveled from the planning board to the pinnacle of professional football. A mere half-dozen years after Joe Robbie, a lawyer and an itinerant politician, and Danny Thomas, the television personality, launched the last expansion franchise in the old American Football League in 1966, the Dolphins defeated the Washington Redskins, 14–7, in Super Bowl VII to become the best team in professional football. If there was one player who best typified the Dolphins' journey through the football stratosphere, it was Lawrence Richard Csonka; a powerful fullback, he was a veritable Gibraltar to the team, a stoic, calm, unflinching eye to the whirling, cleated hurricane.

But like the Dolphins themselves, Larry Csonka did not overwhelm the National

UPI
Jumps over Mark Lomas, Jets' defensive end, and keeps going for first down.

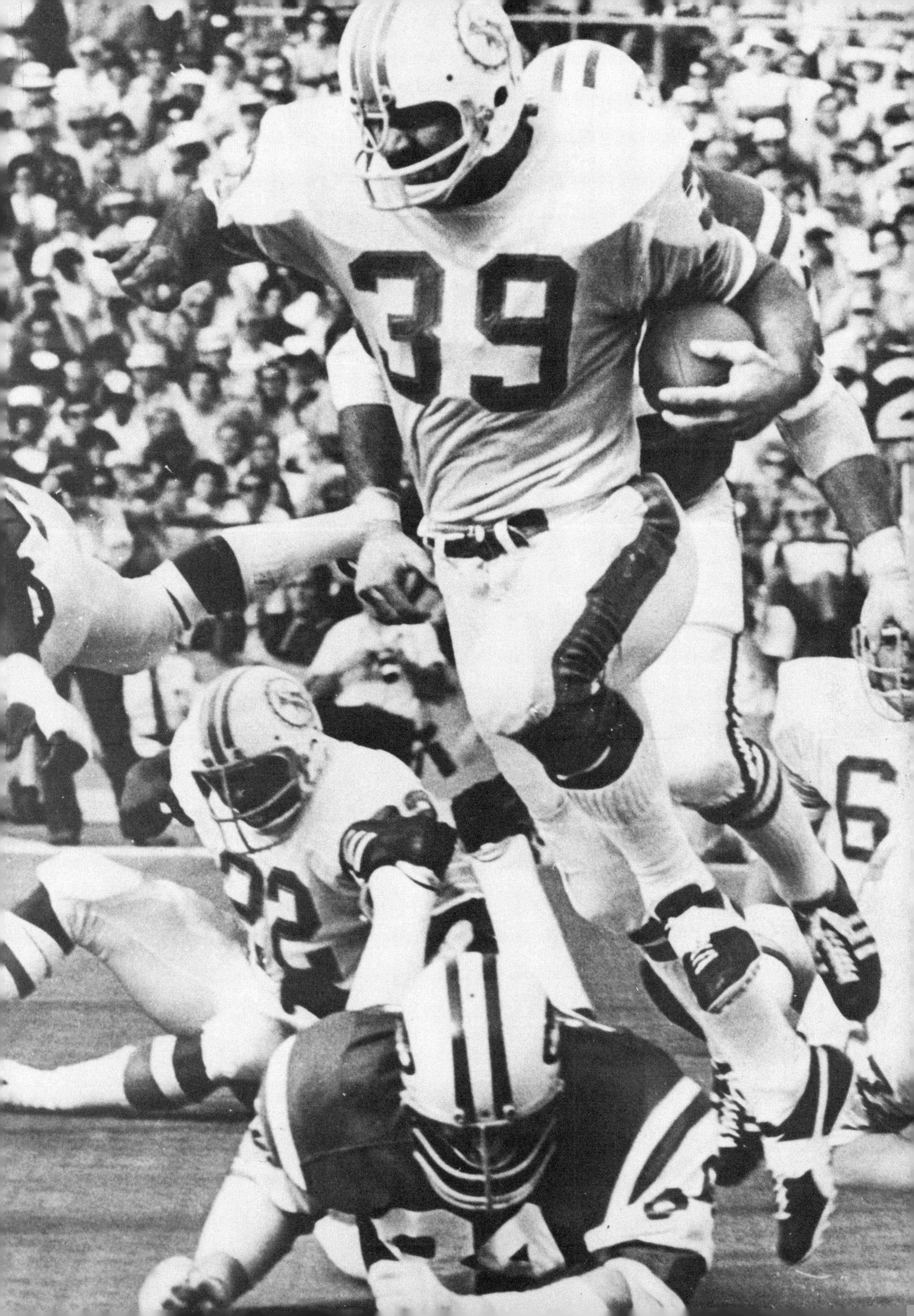

Football League the very first time he laced on his plastic-spiked shoes. In fact, while the team was bobbing in a sea of red ink in its first years, and while management was cutting corners and loading the training table with chow mein, Larry Csonka, fresh out of Syracuse University, was very close to returning to the family farm in Stow, Ohio, to spend his life husking corn and baling hay. Crashing into linebackers had left him with such severe headaches that the team was about to give up on him, lest he risk permanent damage. But Csonka's career was saved by a helmet. The team devised a special helmet for him—it contained a liquified interior to absorb the punishment that Csonka's head had previously absorbed. From then on, the Dolphins and Larry Csonka were literally off and running.

There is Larry Csonka on the field. Look: He is a 6-foot-2-inch, 240-pound block of granite. His full face is dominated by a nose broken nine times over the years. Watch: Two Buffalo safeties at the five-yard line hit Csonka simultaneously from each side. They bounce off. Csonka enters the end zone standing up. Again: Csonka piles into a mountain of Denver defenders, disappears, emerges out the other end to score, dragging defenders. And note: Csonka is the leading rusher in the history of the Miami Dolphins.

Go back to January 16, 1972: The Mi-

Csonka is ready to make his move on muddy field as Jim Langer (62) drives into Bills' defender.

Hard-charging Csonka in action against Jets.

ami Dolphins were playing the Dallas Cowboys in Super Bowl VI in Tulane Stadium in New Orleans. The Dolphins had possession for the second time in the game. Csonka ran 14 yards on a sweep to the right to earn Miami its first down of the game and put the Dolphins on the Dallas 46-yard-line—"good field position," as the cliché goes. In the huddle, Bob Griese, the Miami quarterback, called another play for Csonka; this time it was to be a quick opener up the middle on first down. Griese leaned over Bob DeMarco, the Miami center, called the signals, and took the snap. He whirled and put the ball into Csonka's chest. The handoff was a trifle high, but Csonka headed for his opening, attempting to get control of the ball on the way. He failed; he was hit by a Dallas defensive back and the ball squirted out of his hands. Chuck Howley recovered for Dallas, the Cowboys marched deep into Miami territory, and Mike Clark kicked a nine-yard field goal to give Dallas a 3–0 lead—a lead it never lost en route to a 24–3 victory.

Csonka had not fumbled during that entire season. He had gained over 1,000 yards rushing and had handled the football 235 times, not including 13 pass receptions. After the game, he said that his first fumble of the season had cost the Miami Dolphins the Super Bowl.

"I blew it," he told reporters crowded about him in the locker room. "I was reading the defense before I got the ball. I was a little higher than usual for the handoff, and I think I hit the ball with my knee. If I hadn't done that, it would have been an easy twenty-to-thirty-yard gain. Both tackles were stunting, and we got a good block on the linebacker. That play could have given us the momentum, but it gave it to Dallas, instead. I was hoping the defense would stop them, but the damage was already done."

One year later: The Miami Dolphins were playing the Washington Redskins in Super Bowl VII in the Los Angeles Memorial Coliseum. The Dolphins had not lost a game in a year; they had compiled the first undefeated season in modern NFL history, winning 14 regular-season games and two playoff games. The fumble in Super Bowl VI had not haunted Larry Csonka for long. During 1972, he was the second-best ground-gainer in the American Football Conference and the fourth-best in the National Football League. His statistics: 213 attempts, 1,117 yards gained, six touchdowns scored. He averaged 5.2 yards every time he carried the football.

In that Super Bowl game against Washington, Csonka was the game's leading rusher with 112 yards, nine short of the Super Bowl record set by Matt Snell of the New York Jets in the 1969 game, and he had the longest single gain of the day, a 49-yard run in the fourth period. After the game, in the midst of locker-room pandemonium, Csonka said: "This was probably the best game of my career. But I'll tell you something: I knew I'd have a good game. I was confident. The fumble [the year before] was a fluke. I just knew something like that wouldn't happen again."

* * *

Larry Csonka's confidence might be traced back to a childhood of farm chores and football in Stow, near Akron, Ohio. His father, Joseph, worked at the Goodyear tire plant as well as working the 18-acre spread. Larry Csonka will tell you that his father made him hoe beans "until I wanted to hit him with the hoe," and as punishment, made him kneel on corncobs. He will also tell you that he and his brother slept in a rough-board attic where it was so cold, "I could watch my breath go the length of the room. I had a runny nose the first 10 years of my life."

"I hated that farm until I was old enough to know better," he said. "Now I think how rewarding it was 'growing things,' having animals. Hey, there was a creek and about 20 dogs running around, and we chased woodchucks and climbed trees to get baby crows for pets. It was a beautiful way to grow up. Besides, all the work made me tough."

The Csonkas—uncles, cousins and other relatives—were known around Stow as a physical bunch. "If my father liked you, he hit you on the arm. If he didn't like you, he was also liable to hit you. He was always in great shape," said Larry. "He's 55 now, and he's still got a 34-inch waist. And he can hit you quicker than you can think about it."

Larry Csonka weighed 150 pounds when he was 12 years old. By the time he was a high school junior, he had tried every position in football, including quarterback. "There was something about throwing the ball. I didn't want to turn it loose." His high school games in Stow were memorable as much for the fights in the stands as they were for the play on the field.

Csonka's wife, Pam, was his high school sweetheart and she joined him at Syracuse University. When he was a sophomore, Coach Ben Schwartzwalder had converted him from a fullback to a middle linebacker. "Biggest mistake I ever made," said Schwartzwalder. Csonka was later converted back to fullback. "Smartest move I ever made," said Schwartzwalder.

A Syracuse tackle named Gary Bugenhagen had told Csonka that he should strengthen his forearms by banking them into things. Csonka was envious of the size of Bugenhagen's forearms. That summer Schwartzwalder got a call from Larry Csonka's father. He said to please get Larry out of his house because he was "knocking down the walls."

"Actually," insists Csonka, "it was only one wall, and it was coming down anyway. I used to leave a couple hundred pounds of weights on my bed. My mother would raise hell. She couldn't lift them off to make the bed."

But before he graduated from Syracuse, Csonka had broken all of the Syracuse rushing records of Jim Brown, Ernie Davis, Jim Nance, and Floyd Little. "I'm not really in their class," he will say today. "I just carried the ball more." When he broke the last of Little's records, the officials stopped play to give him the ball. Csonka flipped it to the sidelines. "I didn't know what they were doing," he recalled. "I thought the ball was defective or something."

Csonka's first training camp with the Dolphins was a traumatic one for him. George Wilson was the Miami coach then, and he was a traditionalist who believed that rookies were made to suffer. Csonka, the draft choice, was the biggest target. He suffered most. The veterans called him "The Lawnmower" for his peculiar lock-kneed, low-to-the-ground running style. They not only made him sing his school song, they made him sing *every* school song. They sent him out for sandwiches at two in the morning. They did not get him drunk one night, as is the custom, but took him out and got him intoxicated 10 nights in a row.

"It was," Csonka declared in somewhat of an understatement, "getting to be unbearable."

But things changed rapidly for Csonka and the Dolphins early in 1970 when the Dolphins enticed Don Shula to leave the Baltimore Colts and become their head coach. Shula had the no-nonsense attitude of a Parris Island drill sergeant. Csonka remembered the first Shula camp:

"When Shula first took over, I watched him for a couple days and listened to his yelling, and I said to myself, 'Oh, no, what is this?' I was a regular and here he was, screaming at me, 'All right, Csonka, dammit, if you can't make the play right, then

I'll get somebody in there who can.' At first, I hated it. Then I got to thinking, 'What if I was the second-team fullback and the guy ahead of me wasn't putting out, and the coach wasn't saying a word, ignoring the whole thing?' I'd be damn good and mad about it, and I'd probably be wondering, what kind of coach do we have? That sort of thing would quickly infect the whole team; it would spread like cancer. The result, of course, would be a lot of sulking and dissension. And losing. I came away admiring Shula in that respect; he made it clear to each and every one of us that nobody was fooling him, and that nobody was going to get away with anything.

"If nothing else, Shula proved to us one very important thing in a very short time. He was the boss."

With Shula orchestrating things from the sidelines, and with Csonka and Jim Kiick, his close friend, combining for a devastating ground game on the Orange Bowl turf, the Dolphins surprised everybody during the 1970 season by reaching the American Conference playoffs. But they lost in the first round to the Oakland Raiders, 21–14. They ended the season with a 10–5 won-lost record, a complete turnaround from the 3–10–1 mark of the year before.

Then came 1971. The Dolphins won the AFC title before losing to Dallas in Super Bowl VI. But 1972 was *the* year; no team in the history of professional football had ever won the Super Bowl and also finished the season with an undefeated record. And now that he is a full-fledged star, Larry Csonka can no longer go through life anonymously. His image as a flesh-eating monster of a running back has spawned a large collection of Larry Csonka "stories."

A Larry Csonka story: One night, Larry Csonka was sleeping in a tent while on a camping trip in high school. The woods were dark and quiet. But Csonka was awakened by a strange sound outside his

UPI
Houston Oilers gang up on Csonka with safety John Charles (25) at left in 1972 game.

tent. He got up and looked out. An inquisitive black bear was sniffing nearby. Csonka elbowed the bear in the belly and the intruder fled. When asked about the story, Csonka merely smiled.

"It was nothing special," he said. "It was a small bear."

There were stories, too, that Larry Csonka possessed a rather violent temper. "Untrue," he said.

"The only time I get mad off the field is, well, like when I get up in the middle of the night for a glass of water and I step on a sharp toy left by one of my little boys. Then I get excited. I jump around and holler.

"Or like when my car stalled three times in heavy traffic. The third time, I punched the dashboard. I broke the air conditioner. I also cut my hand open. I was bleeding all over the dash. I just sat there for 15 minutes, feeling like a fool."

But Larry Csonka is opinionated, more than most football players. An example:

"I don't like playoffs. Playoffs can be lethal. Even though we made the playoffs in 1970 as the best second-place team, I don't think any second-place team belongs in the playoffs. If Pete Rozelle wants any suggestion from me—I doubt that he'd listen too attentively—I would reward the teams with the best records by giving them a bye in the first round before meeting the winners of the games in the other two divisions for the conference championships. The winners in each conference would then go to the Super Bowl.

"When the playoffs are not lethal, they are exhausting. Look at our game with Kansas City for the Super Bowl. We won, 27–24, in the second sudden-death overtime period. I was never so tired in my life. When I weighed myself afterwards, I had

Larry Csonka successfully pivots away.

lost 18 pounds."

Perhaps the only thing about Larry Csonka that is not exaggerated, however, is his capacity to endure pain. He has said many times that the only thing he dislikes about professional football is getting up on Monday mornings; sometimes his wife, Pam, has to help him to the breakfast table.

"No matter what your style, you have to take a beating if you're a running back," he said. "If you're small and quick, it might catch up to you all at once, or if you're like me, you might prefer to get it in regular doses, but sooner or later the bill collector comes.

"It's all in the game. I'm no masochist, but I wouldn't want it any other way. I want to be physically involved. I don't want to be in a game where all you've done is throw the ball and don't feel a thing on Monday. Maybe it's a way of letting off steam, I don't know, but afterwards, Jim Kiick and I can relax at a party till five in the morning, just sitting in a corner, Kiick with that empty look on his face, not saying anything. But, hey, I *like* people. I present the image of being a brute, of knuckles dragging. I've had people hesitate to come up to me because they weren't sure what I'd do. I hate that. They don't know me.

"I love the game, that's all. I complain, but I love the whole thing, the total experience. Mind and body. And the result is right there at the end. Running backs figure to last four to six years. The lucky ones last eight or 10. I'd like to go 15. And the only thing that troubles me is that I won't be able to play forever."

Dr. Herbert Virgin, the Dolphins' team physician, has found Csonka to be "an extremely stubborn individual." In return for his advice, Dr. Virgin has learned to expect such rejoinders as, "I'll get over it" [broken nose, sprained knee, etc.] or, "I ain't going to the hospital, and that's final." In 1968, Csonka suffered a concussion in a collision with a Bengal linebacker. For weeks afterwards, the severe headaches he experienced as a rookie returned. His career was thought to be in jeopardy again. A neurosurgeon suggested he reevaluate his occupation. Knocked unconscious again in a game at Miami, Csonka came to on the sidelines to find Dr. Virgin hovering over him and a photographer standing on his hand. He told the photographer to get the hell off his hand. Dr. Virgin called for a stretcher and an ambulance. Csonka got to his feet. "I'm not going to be carried off in front of all those people," he said. "I'm going out the way I came in or I'm not going." Dr. Virgin threw up his hands and followed Csonka to the dressing room.

Another Larry Csonka story: His wife, Pam, was out on the tennis court when little Paul Csonka came crying for attention over a slightly bloody mouth. Pam took a quick look and said to the six-year-old, "Just dab it with something. In this family, you have to learn to live with pain."

			RUSHES				RECEPTIONS				SCORING	
Year	Team	G.	Att.	Yds.	Avg.	TDs	No.	Yds.	Avg.	TDs	TDs	Pts.
1968	Miami	11	138	540	3.9	6	11	118	10.7	1	7	42
1969	Miami	11	131	566	4.3	2	21	183	8.7	1	3	18
1970	Miami	14	193	874	4.5	6	11	94	8.5	0	6	36
1971	Miami	14	195	1,051	5.4	7	13	113	8.7	1	8	48
1972	Miami	14	213	1,117	5.2	6	5	48	9.6	0	6	36
Totals		64	870	4,148	4.8	27	61	556	9.1	3	30	180

UPI

Speeds up against Los Angeles Rams' Phil Olsen (72), Coy Bacon (79), and Deacon Jones (75).

Larry Brown

Larry Brown

by Murray Chass

When Larry Brown was growing up, his mother thought he might become an artist. "He could look at your face and make a beautiful sketch," Mrs. Lawrence Brown, Sr., recalls.

She was only slightly amiss in her thinking. The eldest of her three sons hasn't become an artist in the image of Rembrandt and Picasso. He doesn't paint pictures on canvas; he himself is a picture. But no still-life painting is he; rather, he's flowing action, a blur of burgundy and gold against a green landscape.

He's a picture that 25 other collectors would pay much to own, but he's the property of the Washington Redskins and they exhibit him anywhere from 14 to 17 Sundays each fall and winter. They don't hang him on a wall (although there are many people known as defensive players who

UPI
Leads attack against Atlanta Falcons.

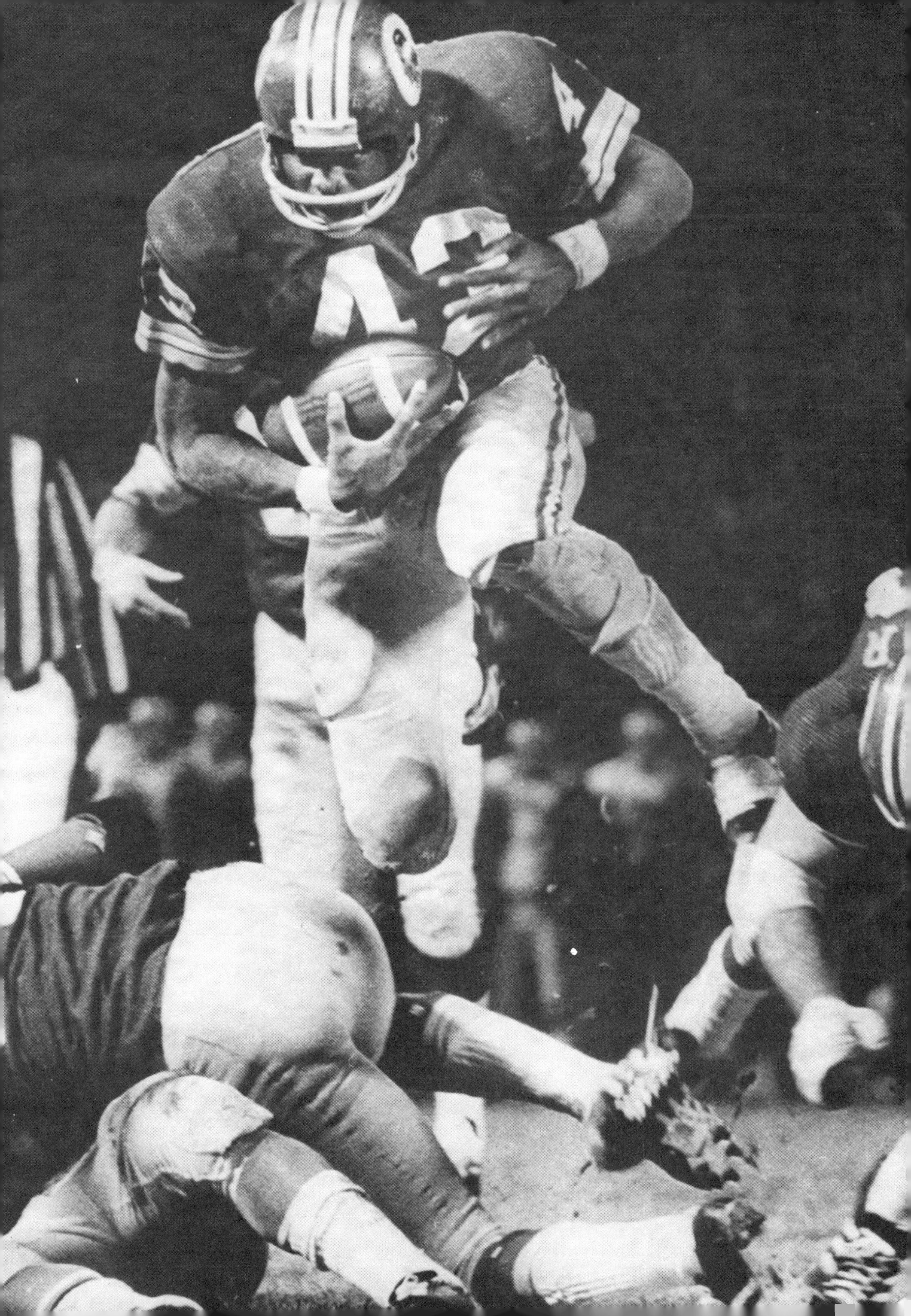

would prefer to have him there), but rather they unleash him to run through, around, and over the team on the other side of the line of scrimmage.

Larry Brown has been so successful at that task that in his first four seasons as a pro running back, he achieved something only two other players had done in NFL history: gain more than 4,000 yards rushing. His four-year total was 4,177, to be exact, which exceeded Cookie Gilchrist's 4,010, but trailed Jim Brown's 5,055.

Brown, a product of the Pittsburgh ghetto known as the Hill District, reached the 4,000-yard plateau in the tenth game of 1972, a Monday night contest against the Atlanta Falcons. That evening, Larry Brown, Sr., watched the game on television with 300 other workers in a recreation room at a railroad yard near Pittsburgh.

"When Larry got the 4,000 yards and they stopped the game to give him the ball, all the men in that room stood up and cheered," says the elder Brown, a crew-caller for the railroad. "They all wanted to shake my hand. No man alive could have been prouder."

If Vince Lombardi were alive, he, too, would have beamed with pride over the success Brown has forged with a determination rarely found in a player. For it was Lombardi who in only one year started Brown on his way toward the top of the hill, a hill far different from the one on which he grew up.

Having escaped the ghetto by winning a scholarship to Dodge City Junior College and then one to Kansas State for his final two years, Brown found himself drafted in the eighth round by the Redskins. But he didn't want to go to Washington; he preferred to try pro football in Canada.

Not even Lombardi could change his mind. It took a black Redskin scout, Bob White, to ease Brown's fears that (1) he would be swallowed up in Washington's ghettos (White lived in a beautiful house in northeast Washington), and (2) his size (5-feet-11, 195 pounds) wouldn't hamper his effectiveness in the NFL. "He told me I could make the club," Brown says now. "He made me feel that I could start for the Redskins."

Once Brown signed with the Redskins, Lombardi took over and began molding him into one of the toughest rookie backs to come along in a long time.

"I was never a glamour back and I knew I wouldn't make it overnight," relates Brown, who at Kansas State first was a blocking back and then a running back in a pass-dominated offense. "I knew I would have to work harder and harder because there were a lot of backs in camp. I knew I had to impress the coaches every day. Then Coach Lombardi began praising me. But as unusual as that was, I knew he wasn't satisfied about something because he kept bringing in more backs. So I kept trying harder, and later on he started picking on me, and that's when I figured I had it made. By picking on me, I felt he was treating me like the veterans, and that made me feel good. I figured I was gaining his respect."

Brown, however, also was gaining Lombardi's wrath and his puzzlement. The wrath emerged when Brown kept dropping passes. To eradicate that problem, the coach handed Brown a football and told him to carry it with him for a week wherever he went, even to church and to bed. Brown didn't drop many passes after that.

But the other problem was more serious, one that Brown didn't even realize existed. Lombardi noted that his prize pupil was consistently late getting off with the snap of the ball, but he couldn't figure out why. Finally, he told Brown to get a hearing test.

"A hearing test?" Brown responded. "Look, coach, I'm probably slow getting off because I'm trying to learn the system and trying to read the defenses at the same time."

Lombardi nodded and smiled. "Get a hearing test," he repeated.

So Brown got a hearing test and discovered he was nearly deaf in his right ear, which meant that whenever he stood to the left of the quarterback, he had difficulty picking up the signals. As a result, he generally had to wait until the ball was snapped before he could start.

To solve that problem, Lombardi ordered a special helmet for Brown, one in which a receiver was placed in the right side and a speaker on the left, with connecting wires running across the top of the player's head. The results said perhaps as much for Lombardi's brilliance as any of the championships he won with the Green Bay Packers.

It comes as no surprise that Brown should say of the man who was his coach for only one year, "He has been the most influential man in my life."

The ghetto, of course, also has been a great influence in Brown's life. Born in the small town of Clairton, Pennsylvania, on September 19, 1947, Brown moved to Pittsburgh's Hill District when he was a boy. There was no rougher neighborhood in the city, a fact attested to by the games the youngsters played. In baseball games, for example, no one would quit and go home early. "If they did," Brown recalls, "everyone on both teams would have a chance to punch the quitter in the stomach. I never risked quitting."

Perhaps that's why Brown never quits now, why he runs and runs and runs, no matter how often the Redskin quarterbacks hand him the ball, and why on those runs he won't go down until he has grabbed every yard, every inch that it is humanly possible for him to grab.

It was on such a play that Larry made an old teammate of Jim Brown revise his thinking about the difference between the great J.B. and all the other runners in the National Football League.

"Larry took a short pass in a game against Dallas, looked at the sideline marker, surged and got a first down," relates Mark McCormack, who blocked for

UPI
Larry Brown finds opening in New York Giants' line as Charley Harraway (left) blocks Larry Jacobson and Paul Laaveg holds off Ron Hornsby.

Jim Brown for six years before becoming an assistant coach at Washington. "Jim had that same knowledge of the yardsticks. A lot of guys will figure they've done their job, but these two work for that first down.

"I always felt that Jim was the greatest running back I've ever seen. But I've had to qualify that statement. I don't think anybody has a bigger heart, is a better competitor, or plays with more desire or toughness than Larry Brown."

As a rookie in 1969, Brown was tough enough to gain 888 yards and make the Pro Bowl squad. In 1970, he made the Pro Bowl again while leading the league with 1,125 yards rushing, which also made him the first player in Redskin history to reach the 1,000-yard mark.

He slipped slightly the following season, falling 52 yards short of 1,000, but he still was a unanimous all-pro selection. Then came 1972, when he rushed for 1,216 yards (two missed games because of leg injuries that kept him from winning the rushing crown), and was named the NFL's Player of the Year as he led the Redskins to the Super Bowl.

His most productive game that year was in Yankee Stadium against the New York Giants when he ran for 191 yards, a career high, caught two passes for 42 yards, and scored two of the 12 touchdowns he amassed during the season. The following week, the other New York team, the Jets, held him to 48 yards on the ground, but he caught three passes, including a one-yarder from Bill Kilmer that he converted into a touchdown by running an additional 88 yards.

The Jets, for some reason, generally have had good success in stopping the league's top runners—at least, on handoffs and not passes from the quarterback—but the Giants had no such luck against this particular runner in his 29 carries.

"We hit him so hard a couple of times I was surprised to see him get back on his feet," notes Jack Gregory, the Giants' fine lineman who led the league in quarterback sackings in 1972. "But he got up and kept running. We couldn't stop him."

Kilmer and Sonny Jurgensen have watched in awe as Brown burst through the smallest hole, darted past a linebacker,

Giants' Spider Lockhart (left) and Ron Hornsby watch Brown take off again.

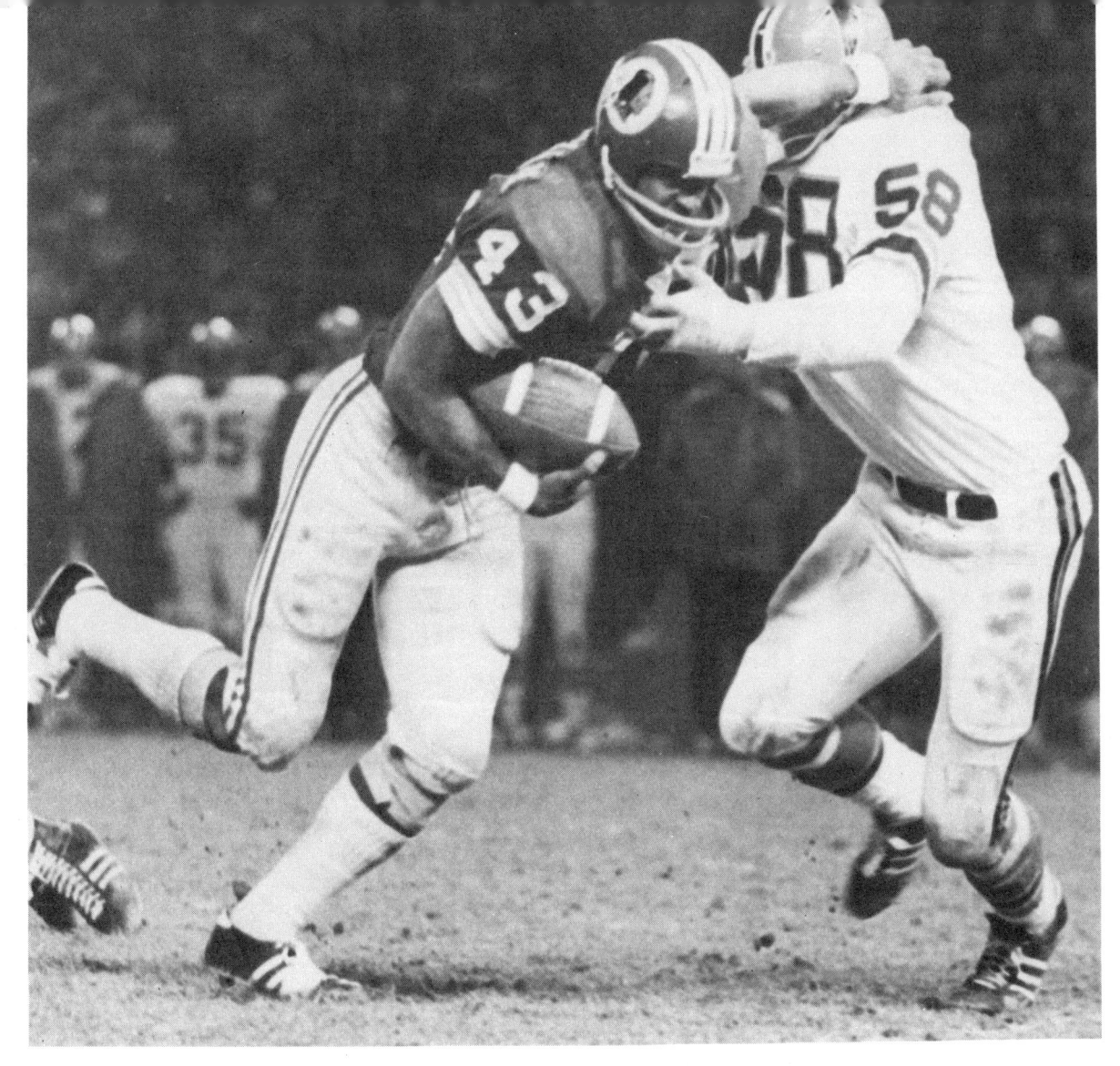

Larry Brown pushes away from Don Hansen of Falcons and makes a sizable gain.

and reached the secondary before another linebacker or a safety made a bone-jarring tackle, often the only type of tackle that brings Brown down.

"Larry takes unreal spills," Kilmer says. "I cringe everytime he goes down and wonder if he'll be able to get up."

"Brown is so intense all the time," adds Jurgensen. "He's not only a scary runner, taking those horrible spills time after time, but he's also a scary blocker. He goes into people to block for Charlie Harraway and I swear he's going to kill someone—either the other guy or maybe himself."

Brown learned the fine art of blocking (Jim Brown frequently was criticized for his lack of blocking effort) as a junior at Kansas State, where he transferred after two relatively unhappy years at Dodge City Junior College.

To begin with, he went to Dodge City because that was about the only place he could get a scholarship. He had received other offers, but he had rejected them because he was considering staying home to help his parents, who were having financial difficulties. Then, when he finally decided that the best way he could help them, in the

Larry Brown confronts Bob Bryant of Vikings as Carl Eller (81) approaches.

long run, was by going to college, the best his football coach at Schenley High School could do was arrange for an offer from Dodge City.

However, when he arrived at the school, he found that the coach who had promised the scholarship had left and the new coach told him he would have to make the team before he could receive aid. He made the team and played well, but he still wasn't satisfied. "I didn't like the situation I was in," he recalls. "The blacks really weren't together, so I thought it would be best to go to a school where I would be more comfortable."

As he was visiting different schools to find one he liked, he learned that Leroy Montgomery, his coach at Dodge, had been named freshman coach at Kansas State. Montgomery advised him to go there for a better chance to play pro football.

"I never had thought about playing pro ball until then," Brown says.

Even after he spent two years at Kansas State, few people thought of the possibility of Larry playing as a pro, but the Redskins did and now they have a player who threatens to be one of the all-time greats.

Comparisons with Jim Brown are inevitable, and Larry Brown is flattered by them.

"As a kid, I used to watch Jim Brown, and I consider any comparison with him a compliment," he says. "Any kid anywhere would consider being compared to him a childhood dream. But let me be myself. Let me succeed or fall on my face as Larry Brown without being compared to others. I just want to be my own man."

Not too many children of the Pittsburgh ghetto known as the Hill get to be their "own man." Many don't even survive long enough to become men.

"It's a rough neighborhood and you had to be rough to survive," Brown says. "Everybody you associated with you had to say the right thing all the time. One little thing you said wrong and you'd get into an argument. But I didn't have very many fights; I can remember four or five. I got along with everybody."

The only people Brown doesn't get along with now are the people who play defense for the Redskins' opponents. Based on the first several thousand yards Brown has gained, that animosity promises to exist for some time to come.

UPI

In 1972 NFC title game, Mel Renfro of Cowboys stretches to try to bring down Larry Brown. Dave Edwards, Dallas linebacker, moves into play.

Year	Team	G.	RUSHES Att.	Yds.	Avg.	TDs	RECEPTIONS No.	Yds.	Avg.	TDs	SCORING TDs	Pts.
1969	Wash.	14	202	888	4.4	4	34	302	8.9	0	4	24
1970	Wash.	13	237	1,125	4.7	5	37	341	9.2	2	7	42
1971	Wash.	13	253	948	3.7	4	16	176	11.0	2	6	36
1972	Wash.	12	285	1,216	4.3	8	32	473	14.8	4	12	72
Totals		**52**	**977**	**4,177**	**4.3**	**21**	**119**	**1,292**	**10.9**	**8**	**29**	**174**

UPI
Demonstrates his All-Pro form in 1972 Jets' game.

O. J. Simpson

O. J. Simpson
by George DeGregorio

When O. J. Simpson was a youngster on the ghetto streets of San Francisco, rumbling with gangs and stealing hubcaps, his biggest asset was his speed. He could run faster than anyone around, even the cops. He was big, strong and agile, and when he tried out for football at Galileo High School he dreamed of becoming another Jim Brown. It was not so wild a dream.

Four years after his graduation from Galileo, Orenthal James Simpson (wearing No. 32, the same number Jim Brown wore), was being hailed as the greatest college running back ever to put on a pair of cleats. Comparisons were being made not only with his boyhood idol, but with Harold ("Red") Grange, George McAfee, Hugh McElhenny, Gale Sayers and others.

He had just completed a record-smashing

UPI

Plunges into the Chiefs' line as Curley Culp prepares to meet him.

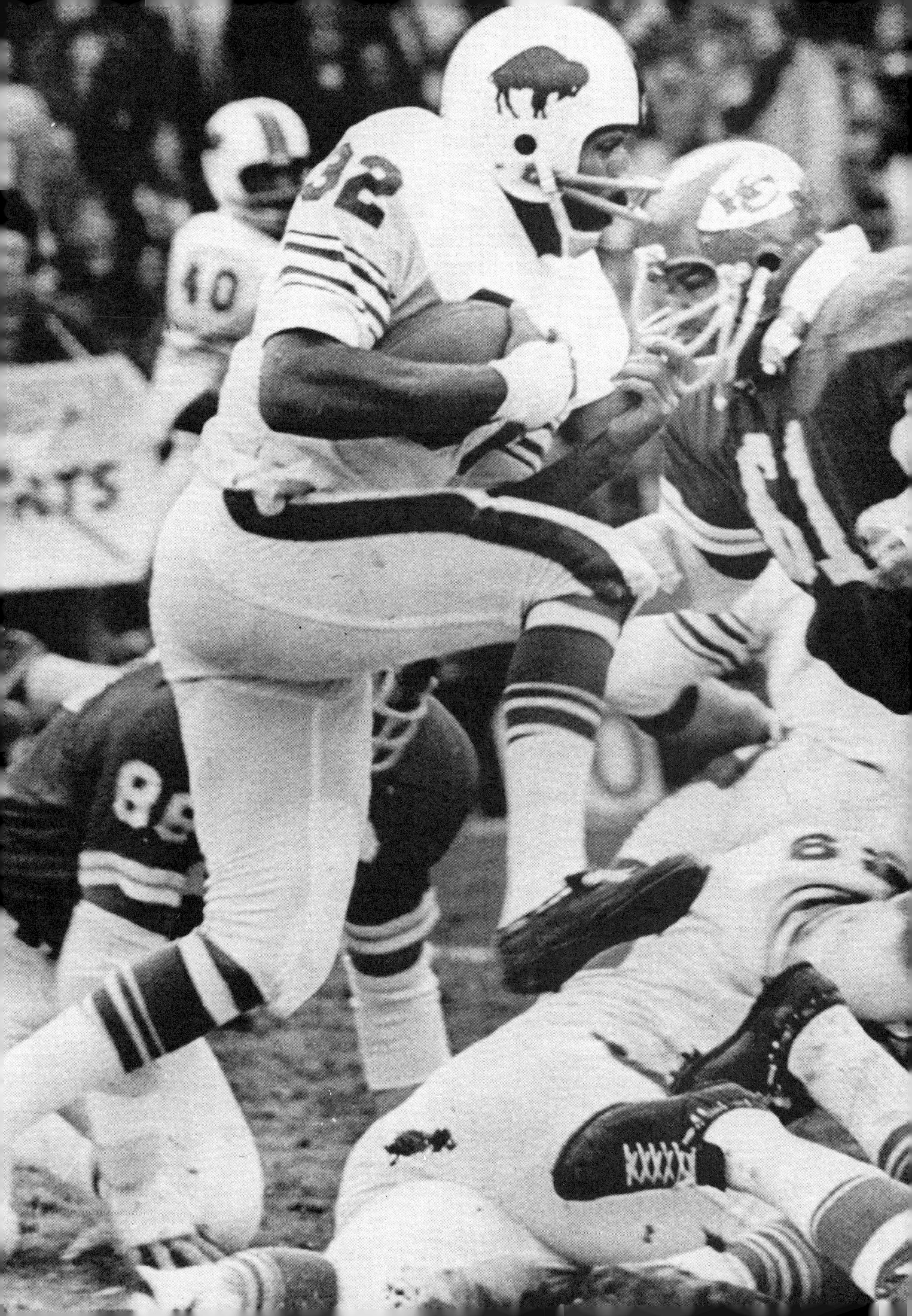
32
10

season with the Trojans of Southern California, rushing for a National Collegiate mark of 1,709 yards in 355 carries and had scored 22 touchdowns. He had won the 1968 Heisman Trophy, awarded to the best player in college football; he was everybody's all-American and he had become the No. 1 pro draft choice, with rights to him as the most sought-after college player going to the Buffalo Bills.

His long runs and explosive power had earmarked him for superstardom. He had led the Trojans to the Rose Bowl twice, and once to a national championship. In two seasons at Southern Cal, he carried 621 times for 3,124 yards and 33 touchdowns, and had averaged just over 5 yards every time he ran with the ball.

If Jim Brown was considered pro football's greatest workhorse, Simpson was his counterpart in college. O. J. carried the ball 30 to 40 times a game for the Trojans and his coach, John McKay, was called a slave driver for using him so much.

"He doesn't belong to a union. He can carry the ball as many times as we want him to," was the way McKay justified his tactics. After all, the Trojans, with O. J. ripping the opposition apart, had won 18 games, tied one, and lost one during his career.

"Some people wondered how come I didn't get more tired than I did," O. J. once explained in an interview. "I got tired. No one will ever know how tired I got. It's funny, but sometimes I'd run better tired. Fresh, early in a game, I'd try to be too cute. I'd think my runs. And the bumps would really hurt. But by the second half, I'd be used to the bruises, and I'd be weary, and I'd just run, natural-like."

The comparisons with the great running backs came from all fronts, even before Simpson stepped on the field as a pro.

"He has to be one of the great ones. He's a threat to go all the way every time he has the ball. He's not as big as Jimmy Brown was, but you have to think about him all the time like you did with Brown," said Weeb Ewbank, coach of the New York Jets. "He's a lot like Sayers. He can turn it on and go, and he reminds me of another back the Bears had—Willie Gallimore. He's got that same stop-and-go style, but he's got a wider base when he runs. He's a quick starter and stopper. Get him one-on-one, you're lucky to stop him."

But to Simpson, even as a youth, life was a challenge, a test to find an identity, one he would be happy with. His path to superstardom among the pros was not strewn with laurel wreaths, although there were plenty of dollar bills. He had been drafted and signed—after prolonged legal hassling —by a team with pro football's poorest record. He would have to display his talents and win his accolades with a chronic loser.

He grew up on Connecticut Street in the Patero Hill section of San Francisco. "It was not the biggest or poorest or most explosive ghetto in the United States," he wrote in his book, *O. J., The Education of a Rich Rookie*, "but it didn't have to be. It still had all the problems and hustles and pain necessary to shape—or twist—the personality of every kid in it. The ghetto makes you want to hide your real identity —from cops, from teachers, and even from yourself."

He was a reluctant student in high school, and when he graduated he wasn't certain what his next move would be. He thought of enlisting in the Army, but through the advice of coaches and friends (and a girl friend—Marguerite Whitley, whom he married in his first year at Southern California, he decided to enroll and play football at San Francisco City College. His exploits there got him to USC, where he became the most publicized player in the country and acquired the nickname, "Orange Juice," an appropriate sobriquet in

UPI
Simpson tries to hurdle Colts' Charlie Stukes; at right is Reggie McKenzie.

view of his great consumption of the drink on and off the field and its obvious application of his initials.

His first pro coach was John Rauch, who preferred a predominantly passing game to a grind-it-out attack. Rauch's reaction to Simpson's workhorse duties at USC gave indication that with Buffalo things would be different for O. J.

"That's not my style," Rauch said. "I couldn't build my offense around one back, no matter how good he is. It's too easy for the pros to set up defensive keys. O. J. can be a terrific pass receiver, and we expect him to block, too."

The Bills' quarterback, Jack Kemp, was of the same mind as his coach. "I just don't think you could run a back 30 times a game consistently in pro football. The best runner I ever played with as a pro was Paul Lowe of San Diego. We'd run him 15 to 18 times and count on him breaking loose once or twice. O. J. will probably run outside more than inside, and, of course, we'll use him in our passing game."

Those who knew O. J. were aware of his intense pride. He believed strongly that he was as good as any pro, that he had all the ingredients to be a superstar and be well paid for it. It was more than vanity.

Even before he signed with the Bills, he had made a dramatic financial breakthrough strictly on his record as a college player. Chevrolet gave him a $250,000 con-

UPI
Patriots are on top of this play and Ed Philpott forces O. J. Simpson back.

How do you stop a tornado?

O. J. rams his way through in typical fashion.

tract for his endorsement of its cars. He was required to appear at auto shows, make television commercials, and in general lend his name to Chevrolet. Besides, he already had in his pocket (while his agent was negotiating with the Bills) a contract with the American Broadcasting Company to act as a sports commentator. A contract with Royal Crown Cola was also being discussed, although it would not be finalized until the season was under way. In all, the off-field enterprises, it was estimated, would yield him $650,000 over a period of years. Simpson felt a deep need to justify all this on the pro gridiron. "I have to be better than good," O. J. said.

It became his motto, the driving force he needed to keep reminding himself that his talent was genuine and the predictions about his becoming a pro superstar were not a fantasy.

"Years ago I used to watch Hugh McElhenny and then Jim Brown most," he said. "McElhenny was the smoothest and

153

UPI

Raiders' Otis Sistrunk manages to get a hand on Simpson, but O. J. eludes him.

the real master at following blockers. People think Brown ran over people, but he glided right by, and when they got to him, he broke them off with his strength. I can't do some of the things Brown could do because he was 228 pounds and I'm not, but I can do most of the things most good backs can do."

When the 6-foot-2-inch, 208-pound Simpson reported to Buffalo for his first training-camp session, he was given the VIP treatment. He received a kiss from Miss Buffalo, the keys to the city from the Mayor, and the cheers of 2,500 fans waiting for him at the Greater Buffalo International Airport. It was an unusual welcome for a raw rookie—one who was worth almost a million dollars even before he had played his first professional game. Buffalo and its fans were hungry for recognition.

After he was drafted (Buffalo got the rights on the basis of its 1–12–1 record), O. J. and the Bills waged one of the most bizarre episodes that ever developed over the signing of a pro player. Through his agent, Chuck Barnes, Simpson embarked on a campaign in which he demanded the largest money package ever asked for by a rookie. His terms were $600,000 in salary and a $500,000 loan at 5 per cent interest for investment purposes, both for five years. The negotiations took many twists and turns, and the talks between both sides

UPI
O. J. Simpson displays high knee action as Patriots' Ed Weisacosky closes in.

went on for several months. The sparring was for high stakes, but each side knew it needed the other.

Simpson threatened not to sign, declared he wouldn't mind being traded because he didn't like the cold Buffalo climate in the first place, and would rather play on the West Coast, close to home.

The Bills had a great deal of faith in O. J.'s appeal at the gate; after they drafted him, they scheduled an exhibition game at the Coliseum in Los Angeles, O. J.'s home town. With him they figured they could draw 75,000 fans, without him maybe 30,000. They could recover a good part of his salary on that game alone, to say nothing of his drawing power thereafter.

Simpson, of course, knew he needed a good showcase and image—his value as a public relations ambassador for Chevrolet and as a TV commentator depended greatly on whether he could sustain his image as a super-athlete in the public eye. With these and many other considerations playing a role in the tug of war, Simpson finally agreed to a four-year contract for an estimated $350,000, plus an annuity at age 50.

But it wasn't until the 1972 season, when Coach Lou Saban returned to the helm to guide the Bills, that Simpson was given his head and let loose to show what he could do. Saban, an advocate of the running game, had previously gone to Denver to revitalize the Broncos. There he helped in

There are times when even the mighty must fall.

the development of Floyd Little, a Syracuse star who became one of the league's more talented runners.

Despite playing with an offensive line that was young, inexperienced and injured for virtually most of the campaign, Simpson rushed for 1,251 yards in 292 carries, both Bills' records, to win the National Football League rushing crown. He was named the American Football Conference player of the year by United Press International and by the New York Chapter of the Professional Football Writers Association of America.

The Bills, of course, were still floundering, finishing with a 4–9–1 record, but management, with Saban back to keep Simpson in the groove, was looking ahead to more league-leading seasons from O. J., and possibly a winning combination on the field. In his three previous seasons with the Bills they had not won more than four games in a campaign. The 1969 season, Simpson's first, produced a 4–10 mark. And when he was out with a knee injury after eight games of the 1970 season, they finished with a 3–10–1 record. In 1971, they won only once in the season and lost 13 times.

The Bills were a woefully poor team. Superstar or not, Simpson managed to dis-

Dennis Shaw hands off to O. J., who is already driving forward at full speed.

O. J. starts to fling football to ground after crossing goal line.

Robert L. Smith

tinguish himself and show that he was not merely a college flash in the pan. O. J. was the team-rushing leader each season. During the 1971 season, with Rauch and Kemp sticking to their pass-oriented offense, Simpson utilized his speed as a receiver and caught 21 passes for 162 yards, in addition to rushing for 742 in 183 carries.

The Simpson charisma had grown out of his ability to reel off long gainers. His tremendous speed (he has sprinted 100 yards in 9.4 seconds) and his twisting, snaking style in breaking off tacklers marked him as a runner of unstoppable quality. Among the pro fans and sportswriters it earned him a new nickname, "Mr. Excitement."

Simpson's best single-game rushing effort came in 1972 against the Steelers in Pittsburgh when he ran for 189 yards, including a 94-yard touchdown gallop. The one-game yardage was the best of the year in the AFC. And his self-image of being "better than good" was taking hold—and with his best years ahead of him.

			RUSHES				**RECEPTIONS**			
Year	Team	G.	Att.	Yds.	Avg.	TDs	No.	Yds.	Avg.	TDs
1969	Buffalo	13	181	679	3.9	2	30	343	11.4	3
1970	Buffalo	8	120	488	4.1	5	10	139	13.9	0
1971	Buffalo	14	183	742	4.1	5	21	162	7.7	0
1972	Buffao	14	292	1,251	4.3	6	27	198	7.3	0
Totals		**49**	**776**	**3,178**	**4.1**	**18**	**88**	**842**	**9.6**	**3**

	KICKOFF RETURNS				**SCORING**	
Year	No.	Yds.	Avg.	TDs	TDs	Pts.
1969	21	529	25.2	0	5	30
1970	7	333	47.6	1	6	36
1971	4	107	26.8	0	5	30
1972	1	21	21.0	0	6	36
Totals	**33**	**990**	**30.0**	**1**	**22**	**132**